Companion Workbook to

How to Get Interviews!
Stop Sending Job Search Junk Mail

# How to Win Your 'Inner Game!'

# Update Your Attitude Before You 'Update Your Résumé'

*Donald M. Burrows*

© *2014 Acorn Consulting Inc.*

**Purchasers!**

*Jump-Start Your Job Search!*

*Sign up for Free Orientation Webinar at*

StopSendingJobSearchJunkMail.com

*How to Win Your 'Inner Game' - Update Your Attitude Before You 'Update Your Résumé'*

*(Companion Workbook to How to Get Interviews! Stop Sending Job Search Junk Mail)*

Cover design by Purity_K - www.fiverr.com/purity_k.

Interior design by www.ipublicidades.com

Visit the author's website: www.StopSendingJobSearchJunkMail.com

ISBN: 978-0-9849050-7-2

# Table of Contents

# Dedications

My thanks to **John Locke,** *The New York Times* Best Selling Author, first self-published author to sell one million eBooks on Amazon Kindle, and creator of the four connected and wildly different and entertaining series (Donovan Creed, Gideon Box , Danni Ripper and Emmett Love)

Thank you for sharing your roadmap. How I Sold 1 Million eBooks in 5 Months

My thanks also to **Geoff Bellman,** Organization Development consultant, author of The Consultant's Calling – Bringing Who You Are to What You Do.

I owe Geoff a tremendous debt. Two decades ago, teetering on the brink of leaving Corporate America and going independent, I read *The Consultant's Calling.* I realized he had written my exit strategy blueprint. Graciously meeting with me in 1993, Geoff rendered me speechless with this question: *"What's unique about Don?"* He started me on a 20-year quest to move beyond *"generic"* and into *"unique."*

You're reading one of the answers to his question.

Thank you, sir. That was one hell of a question!

To **William Bridges,** author of Jobshift – How to Prosper in a Workplace without Jobs and Creating You & Co.: Learn to Think like the CEO of Your Own Career. You opened my eyes and my mind to surviving and thriving in what you called a *"dejobbed"* world.

To my good friend **JonScott Williams,** successful user and staunch advocate of my system and contributor to this and earlier books. JonScott gave me the concept of *"Tastefully Boasting"* with your accomplishments.

And to another good friend, **Brent Ward** (www.RubyRed.biz) long-time believer, user and proactive booster. Brent introduced me to the concept of not following *"Boilerplate Herd."*

To **Deborah Drake,** (www.AuthenticWritingProvokes.com) co-author of **Burn Your Résumé! You Need a Professional Profile,** who first suggested the need for a Workbook, And for effortlessly coming up with this critical thought: *"Wouldn't it be horrible to create a résumé that got you an interview, and then give an interview that made them wonder why they brought you in?"*

A heavenly hat-tip to **Napoleon Hill** for contributing so much to the formation of both my values and character. Author of two of my favorite books –Think and Grow Rich and Law of Success – I don't think you'll find a better teacher. The Napoleon Hill Foundation continues his work today.

And finally, my thanks to my young mentor – **Eric Castaneda**, author of Action Mentality and Time Management is a Myth.

I'm in your debt for that insightful, pragmatic and liberating conversation. It solidified my awareness of the *Generic 90%* and the *Motivated 10% of job seekers,* and that has made all the difference.

# Why you should read this book:
# Testimonials from real people
# who got real results

Before you read the Testimonials, let me set the stage.

In this highly niched and CUSTOM labor market, you are sending out **Job Search Junk Mail** if you are distributing THE SAME GENERIC résumé for different positions, EACH WITH SPECIFIC REQUIREMENTS. You're making it ridiculously easy for HR, recruiters and hiring managers to ignore you.

Forever.

The longer you *"see"* yourself and *"present"* yourself as a strand of *"Wandering Generality"* *spaghetti*, blending in with everyone else and not standing out like a *"Meaningful Specific"* MEATBALL, the longer you are responsible for prolonging your unemployment.

**And the really sad part is this:** Each time you never hear back, or get a screening call but are not invited in for an interview, you lose more of your self-confidence, self-esteem and your ability to bounce back from rejection. It gets harder and harder not to take it personally. And down deep, your little voice worries more and gets louder and more fearful.

This book is about **Winning Your Inner Game**. If what you just read in the last two paragraphs is true for you, *you are losing your "Inner Game."*

When you don't get interviews for work you know you are qualified to do, your spirit shrivels and your self-confidence does as well. You probably do what most people do.

For want of a better term, you do **the Same-Old Same-Old**. And it is exactly the wrong thing to do.

You **"Update Your Résumé."** You then send out a bunch more *"Wandering Generality"* résumés that people ignore. And you repeat your deepening cycle of prolonged fear and depression. You are treating the symptom, not the problem.

This **Companion Workbook** to **How to Get Interviews! Stop Sending Job Search Junk Mail** is the key to breaking the cycle by first **"Updating Your Attitude"** then **"Updating Your Résumé."**

When you first update your attitude and begin winning your *Inner Game,* you'll regain the self-esteem and self-confidence you've lost in your failing and flailing search for meaningful work you want to do. You'll get crystal-clear on your **relevant professional accomplishments**, and as you effectively customize your credentials to each opportunity you seek, you'll be an *"Ideal Candidate"* each time you apply – when you stop mass-distributing your generic résumé and only apply where it makes sense for you to apply – where you can be an "IDEAL CANDIDATE" each time you apply.

My D-I-Y résumé-writing system has worked for hundreds of job seekers, solopreneurs, freelancers and managers-in-transition.

Here's what some of them have had to say.

## JOB SEEKERS

"Don Burrows has put a spin on the traditional résumé which, unlike so many others out there, actually works." Jennifer Haga. Business Development Manager. Raleigh, NC

"Don Burrows gets you the attention you deserve by showing hiring managers exactly why they should hire YOU! A Professional Profile will get your phone ringing and will get you that interview." Scott Bell. Creative Director/Producer

"A day after I finished my professional profile and sent it out I received several calls within a few hours for job interviews. . . . If you want to get your dream job, work with Don." Eric Castaneda. Author of *Time Management is a Myth*

"I highly recommend the book to anyone searching for a job, looking at changing careers or just simply searching for a new tool to reformat their current résumé. Have doubts about yourself? Take a good look at your Database of Accomplishments. The positive effects are incredible." Lourdes Tsukada

"Being a transitioning military officer who did not want your typical defense consulting job . . . Don helped me create a profile of transferrable skills that any employer would love to see in an applicant. Don really opened my eyes to all the possibilities in the world." Billy Duke. Former Army Infantry Officer

"Don's Professional Profile process will not only provide you with a resume that will ring your phone, it will prepare you for the follow-up interviews. . . . You will be amazed at the impact you've had on your employers, and yourself." RBS, Customer Voice at Lulu.com

"I tried for three months on my own after graduation to have meaningful contact with companies that might be interested in a recent college graduate with a physics / mathematics degree. . . . Don helped me put together a Professional Profile I have submitted to several companies and while they have not had entry level positions available, they were interested enough to meet with me." Kyle Margolies. Recent College graduate

**This is an unsolicited testimonial. I realize it is lengthy and I hope you'll take the time to read it. I found myself unable to edit it because it speaks to so many facets of my Professional Profile system. And besides, I simply love the story.**

"When I first heard of the "Accomplishment Based Résumé" I thought the idea was novel, but didn't think about it much, as I wasn't looking for employment. When I recently became unemployed, I realized with the unemployment as high as it was, that my résumé would have to stand out somehow. More importantly, I would have to show any future employer why I was worth the wages I was asking for. Trying to condense my skills and abilities into a chronological résumé was painful for me. How could I possibly show a perspective employer that one of my greatest strengths is thinking outside of the box to create real and lasting solutions, when a chronological résumé is exactly that . . . a box.

"So by using Don Burrows' process, I was able to show perspective employers how my mind actually works. I was able to show how I would create a process to accomplish a goal, or how I overcome challenges and interact with people. The epiphany that I had accomplishments that would qualify me for multiple roles in multiple industries was absolutely delightful! The implications of this realization are far reaching for me and have changed the way I view my career.  As cliché as it may sound, I am free, free from the box. I was now able to use my "Accomplishment Database" to submit a unique and polished résumé to companies in any applicable industry in minutes, thereby increasing my visibility and chances of an interview.

"The direct result of following Don Burrows' process was securing an interview with my target company. I was unemployed for a total of 1 week. After I was hired I was told at a later date that my résumé was "the best résumé I have ever seen!" high praise from a former Panasonic Japan exec. This compliment amused me as I had gone from having the worst résumé to "the best" in the length of time it took me to read the book. – Aaron Urban. Journeyman Carpenter. Everett, WA

## FREELANCERS AND SOLOPRENEURS

"Don, I went from tongue-tied to fluently speaking, from *"I don't know what I have to offer"* to *"This is what people gain when they work with me."* The system . . . was challenging but so worth the effort! I am much more confident talking about my services than before." Leona Rehm. SimplyEffectiveCoaching.com

". . . I kept going through the process and discovered more than I had ever thought possible. There I was writing these things about this person that just happened to be me. Don's method is intense, the process gut wrenching, but the results are truly amazing." Susan Straub-Martin. strauberrystudios.com

"Convention is to put as much as possible in a résumé and follow the boilerplate herd. Courageous approaches focus on simplifying a résumé to only those items that are important. Don's wisdom is to consider the things that may not yet even be on the page! And that has made all the difference." Brent Ward. Business Development. RubyRed.biz

"This is something every entrepreneur should do. This system not only brings a clear vision of who you are to your customers … you will amaze yourself by re-discovering all the gifts and talents you bring to your business and customers…" Gerald Grinter, Business Mentor, Insurance Executive and Author. TheArtofWorkingforYourself.com

## EXECUTIVES-IN-TRANSITION

"There is no one I have ever met that brings as much of himself, his humanness and his humanity, to his work as Don Burrows. This is neither conjecture nor hyperbole … this is a personally experienced fact." JonScott Williams. Organizational Generalist / OD Consultant

"My final interview was with the CEO. He said that I was at the top of his list to have interviewed for one reason: *'This is a disruptive résumé. I had to meet the engineer who thinks like this.'* A week later I received an offer." Greg Pease. Director of Engineering. (His *"Disruptive résumé"*/cover letter follow)

# "DISRUPTIVE" RÉSUMÉ AND COVER LETTER

## Education
**Advanced Special Student**
Post Graduate Studies
**27 / 33 hours of Ph.D. in Multiple Autonomous (Robotic) Systems**
**4 of 7 chapters of dissertation**
U of STATE (6 hrs) and U of STATE (21 hrs)
GPA 3.5/4.0 GPA
**Master of Science**
**Mechanical Engineering**
University State Name. GPA: 3.5/4.0.
**Bachelor of Science**
**Mechanical Engineering**
University of State Name
GPA: 2.8/4.0
(GPA: 3.6/4.0 last 60 credit hours)
Dean's List last (5) Semesters

## Computer Related Skills
### Engineering/Technical
Matlab
Simulink
LabView
Maple
CFDesign
Programming:
Visual Basic
C/C++/C#

### Productivity
MS Office Professional
SAP
Modeling/Drafting:
Solid Works
Unigraphics
Microstation
AutoCAD

## Additional Training
US Army Leadership Development
Design for Manufacturing / Assembly
Production Systems Modeling & Analysis
Project Management Institute PMP (174 PDU's)
Quality System Regulation FDA 21CFR820
EEOC / Ethics

## Areas of Special Interest
**System Modeling and Control**
(State Space, Classical)
**Electronic Systems Theory and Design**
**Theory of Combustion**
(Slow Burn and Explosion)
**Robotics** (Controls, Modeling)
**Mechanical Properties of Materials**
(Materials Engineering)
**Dynamics** (Rigid, Multi-Body)

**TOP SECRET Clearance**
**E.I.T. Certified**

---

**OBJECTIVE: Director of Engineering for COMPANY NAME / DIVISION / PRODUCT**, a position requiring significant project management, hardware and software research and development experience, metrics-based people management skills, and a deft touch to mentor and develop staff.

## SPECIAL SKILLS AND ABILITIES

| | | |
|---|---|---|
| Flexible managerial skills and experience to successfully guide, mentor, manage and develop a range of individuals of varying skills, education, age and temperament | Entrepreneurial mindset and the ability to balance multiple projects and priorities, carrying each through to successful completion | Strong sense of personal initiative to resolve bottom line problems, blending theoretical engineering expertise with practical applications |
| Accustomed to managing strict budgets, achieving results within time and budgetary constraints | Expert project management skills and corresponding experience to chart project's course, and adjust as needed | Broad range of engineering, computer, business software and peripherals |

## REPRESENTATIVE PROFESSIONAL ACCOMPLISHMENTS:

NEW PRODUCT DEVELOPMENT:

o Led a three-year engineering and design initiative for the major redesign of the Company Name / Product Name in-vitro diagnostic instrument. (Company)

o Brought engineering and design efforts to completion 25% under budget; The unit price increase resulting from the product enhancements.

o Based upon the perceived value increase, the team was able to sell the unit for 16% more and the sales increased by ~20%, managing customer expectations in the process.

o Directly managed the contributions of six engineers and indirectly lead another 14 engineers and technicians. Partnered with an industrial design firm and manufacturers to reduce expected program costs by over $850K.

o Led knowledge transfer teams from development to production with continued to support product through commercial sales.

**REPRESENTATIVE PROFESSIONAL ACCOMPLISHMENTS (continued):**

- Over a five-year period, led over 30 project teams made up of internal engineers, component vendors and external consultants in development of new products from inception through commercial manufacturing. Developed and managed individual project budgets of up to $2M. Managed product sustainment throughout their lifecycles. In one case, product generated sustained 30% sales increase in its sector.(Company)

- Demonstrated proficiency in development of proof of concept prototypes for mechanical, electrical (including power and PCB design), and embedded system programming. Championed projects through commercial implementation and initial production runs. Supported manufacturing during knowledge transfer phase, making myself available 24/7 by giving select manufacturing technicians my personal cell number.(Company)

EXISTING PRODUCT DEVELOPMENT

- As lead engineer for complex electro-mechanical products generating $1.7B annually, I was responsible for making the initial assessment of equipment problems referred to Engineering. I implemented a root cause analysis approach covering R&D to Implementation. After just two projects using this approach, the company realized over $100K a month savings. (Company)

- I was able to proactively identify obsolesce issues arising from ROHS and REACH legislation which may have prevented the selling of our instruments overseas. I generated a series of projects to address the future problems so that they could be solved in a non-crisis mode. (Company)

RESOURCE MANAGEMENT

- Led program that reduced unit costs due to obsolescence and through product enhancements. Managed development costs and schedule for multi-year efforts, responsible for as many as 12 critical path projects simultaneously. My work saved the organization over $200K each month in ongoing bottom line costs for parts, labor and logistics. (Company)

- For the category of industry, I evaluated new software for use in electrical, instrumentation and process design. The proposed software required $100K in up-front costs and required $125k per year in licensing fees. After spending some time with the software, I found that, because of the overly complicated nature of the program, there was no productivity gain. I demonstrated some simple (and industry standard) techniques would yield significant productivity gains to my internal clients. After documenting the techniques, the company adopted my suggested processes. (Company)

INNOVATION, RESEARCH AND DEVELOPMENT

- Out of personal interest and curiosity, I developed a new manner in which to analyze military systems. My initiative resulted in an increasingly more realistic way to evaluate weapon effects. My research combined statistics, image analysis and materials engineering in a novel approach to the problem. This research attracted the attention of the US military branch leadership and I was asked to present my findings to the Senior Analysts Group (SAG) at the Pentagon and to senior researchers at the Department of Defense Research Centers across the US. The US military branch adopted this approach and it has become the standard approach to deterministically determine weapons effects. As a result of these efforts, I received an award from the three star Commanding General of the US Military Branch / Organization. (US MILITARY ORGANIZATION)

INTERDIVISIONAL COMMUNICATION

- For a production line update for the fiber industry, created an opportunity to automate the process due to structural symmetries. Working with a cross-functional team of engineers and designers, developed process through which a database and set of generic templates were used to automatically generate some 480 production drawings. Once the generic drawing template was agreed upon, the team only needed to input their equipment identification numbers into the database. The system would then generate drawings, and when requested, would plot them for review. This process yielded drawings with nearly 100% accuracy, and saved the project over 10,000 hours in design time. (Company)

MANAGEMENT AND POLICY

- Served as mentor, collaborator and support for peer, junior and senior engineers, providing developmental coaching and training in areas such as Lean Engineering principles and in the use of standard engineering practices. Initiated compliance paperwork to help projects in danger of missing milestones. Occasionally served as internal consultant providing software examples, prototype samples or solutions. These efforts have lead to four promotions. (Company)

- I started Name of Restaurant and Pub in City, State in 2007. Generating over $4M in sales in just 4 years, I managed a staff of 22, was responsible for all legalities of the business, financial reporting and building/maintaining solid government relations at the local, county, state and federal levels. After working a full day, I oversaw the night operations 6 days a week until closing. This work did not have a negative effect upon my engineering responsibilities evidenced by the promotions I received during this time. Sold the business to dedicate more time with family.

CUSTOMER / VENDOR RELATIONS

- I have learned the practical wisdom of cultivating a professional and mutually respectful relationship with my customers and vendors. It is well known that field engineers replace parts until problem goes away, guessing which part solved the problem. Generally, the engineering group receives only an incident report. I have found that through regular communication with field engineers, I could better understand what failure they observed and so could develop better designs. (Company, University of State Name, US Military Organization)

- I engage the fabrication vendors early on in the design process as a habit. In general, their personnel can provide advantageous input which can reduce cost and timelines. Further by getting their buy-in to the design and through regular communications with them, I am also able to negotiate better terms and, often times, receive prototype parts/assemblies at low or no costs with highly aggressive timelines. (Company, University of State Name, US Military Organization)

**RELEVANT PROFESSIONAL HISTORY**
**US MILITARY ORGANIZATION,** Location (Sept. 2009 – Contract End 12/11)
My work impacts on in excess $180M per year for infrastructure and $450M in development opportunities.
  *Deputy Manager / Senior Engineer – Infrastructure and Investment Management / Test and Evaluation*

Providing guidance and oversight of US Military Branch test centers' investment and infrastructure planning. Providing technical guidance, planning, cost estimation, cost tracking and schedule oversight of major investments. Generating budgetary numbers for future costs. Inventory skills and capabilities of Department of Defense R&D test centers. Consult on and provide input to test activities to reduce timelines and costs. Engage in component- and system-level discussions to reduce timelines and assembly costs. Proposal development for new system development. Proposal writing and support to acquire new contract and development opportunities.

**COMPANY** (Formerly Company).  Location (Sept. 2004 – Sept. 2009)
My work impacted on gross sales of over $1.7B per year based upon 2009 earnings.

*Lead Engineer – Global Engineering Research and Development*
Focused on troubleshooting complex electro-mechanical products. Managed interdisciplinary project teams in the US, Germany and an Italian contractor (Company – producer of automation solutions) to analyze causes of failures and the development of product and process enhancements. Also managed interdisciplinary teams responsible for new product development from inception to commercial manufacturing. Developed baseline costs and schedules. Developed pre-production designs for proof of concept efforts. Coordinated technical solutions with Supplier Operations, Marketing, Chemistry and Quality Teams to ensure availability and costs were in line with established standards and customer needs. Interfaced with customers to ensure their needs were understood and to set mutual  expectations. Developed Failure Modes and Effects Analyses (FMEA).

**Project/ Product Life Cycle Management**. Oversaw quality assurance of medical device design (RA/QA).  Maintained compliance with 510(k) submissions. Promptly completed Corrective Actions/Preventative Actions (CAPAs). Design validation, verification and reliability testing.  Development of lean manufacturing SOPs. Development of laboratory capabilities. Developed junior personnel in skills and knowledge resulting in four promotions.

**US MILITARY BRANCH ORGANIZATION.** Location.  (Aug. 2002 – Sept. 2004)
My work impacted $1.8B in materiel development projects.

*Mechanical Engineer (GS-12+)*
Simulation and modeling. Cost vs. Performance trades considered. Developed requirements for current and future systems, developed Key Performance Parameters (KPP) and developed Analysis of Alternatives (AoA). Worked with cross-military teams to develop Operational Requirements Documentation (ORD). Project estimation, planning and technical solutions.

**University of STATE.** Location. (Sept. 2000 –June 2002)
*Research Assistant/Teaching Assistant*
Designed and developed control systems and robotics systems. Modeling and simulation of the physical and electrical systems. Component design. Primary focus: Optimal Control of Multiple Autonomous Unmanned Ground Robots. Developed and executed tests for MAUGVs including cost tracking, schedule, analysis and report. Independent research in the areas of controls and nonlinear dynamics. Provided mentoring to over 80+ undergraduate students in the subjects of Statics and Dynamics. Planning and oversight of capital upgrades to laboratory infrastructure to generate additional capabilities for test and evaluation of research equipment.

**COMPANY.** Location. (Jan. 1999 – Sept. 2000)

*Process Engineer (Reason for leaving: Began full time work on a PhD in Mechanical Engineering.)* Led a team of senior designers, PDMS designers and CAD draftsmen in the design and specification of chemical process lines and factory design. Managed an interdisciplinary team to improve communications and better standardization. On-site installation of equipment. Start-up testing and reporting of system functionality.

**COMPANY.** Location. (Jan. 1994 – Sept. 1999)

*Electrical/Instrumentation/Mechanical Designer*

Electrical, mechanical and instrumentation design. Designed automation systems to improve drafter productivity. Due to high energy and self-motivation, tasked to support projects in jeopardy of missing deadlines or exceeding personnel budget. Field testing and support of system start-up. Worked this position during my undergraduate education as an additional means of support. During this employment, I transferred to the STATE NAME University to complete my education, after having made the transfer, I found that the College would not accept 40 credit hours. After completing a semester there, I transferred back to University of STATE NAME.

**COMPANY.** Location. (Sept. 1997 – Jan. 1998)

*Site Lead/Designer (Reason for leaving: Transferred from NAME OF STATE University to the University of STATE NAME to finish undergraduate degree.)*

In conjunction with plant engineers and technicians, designed the electrical and instrumentation systems of a tank farm for the on-site distillation of acetone and methanol. Appointed by the lead instrumentation engineer to direct the work of 25 electrical and instrumentation contractors.

**In my Spare Time**

*RESTAURANT NAME. Location.* (July 2006 –April 2011)

*Managing Member/Owner*

Managed a staff of up to 22 employees generating sales of over $4 million. Managed vendor interactions for advertising/ marketing, services, equipment and product. Developed and implemented Health, Safety and Environmental policies. Actively drove cost reductions and increased product quality. Developed and implemented HR policies. Developed and implemented Approved Supplier Approval policies. Developed and implemented procurement policy. Managed financial reporting from senior staff members. Managed government relations at the Local, County, State and Federal levels. Assumed legal responsibility for business. Developed and implemented a charitable giving policy which generated over $70K in donations to support research in Breast Cancer, Langerhans Cell Histeocytosis and Leukemia. Sold the business to dedicate more time with family.

**OUTSIDE INTERESTS**

- Family

- Soccer

- Chess

- Strategy games

- Reading – Control Systems, Math

**NAME AND CONTACT DATA**

Ms. First Last
Position
Company
Address
City, State, Zip

Dear Ms. Last Name,

Thank you for inviting me to submit my résumé for the position of Director of Engineering for Company's Product Name line. I am very excited, and the more I compared your requirements with my experience and interests, the more excited I became.

I want you to know right up front that I am not a plodding engineer; rather, I am a forward-thinking engineering leader with a proven track record for delivering high quality products on time and to standards. I have earned a reputation for innovation, rigorous testing procedures, a proactive and hands-on approach to cost reductions, meeting deadlines on large and small scale projects, and ability to lead and develop the engineers and technicians on my projects.

Here is how I compare in terms of what you seek for the position and what I offer:

| YOU SEEK: | I OFFER: |
|---|---|
| 1. Experience to direct all activities related to the research and development of hardware and software products, including creation, analysis, development, prototyping, testing and successful transition to manufacturing | • More than 15 years of experience leading product development teams in a range of industries – chemical, military, and medical – both domestically and internationally and success with transitioning designs from R&D to Manufacturing. |
| 2. Manage the development of the division's full line of products, working with domestic and international operational staffs. | • Proven ability to manage the efforts of a diverse electro-mechanical product line. Strong ability to develop effective, lasting partnerships with all stakeholders with diverse backgrounds. |
| 3. Review, validate, prioritize and allocate resources to manage and resolve problem reports | • Solid track record eliminating production delays without sacrificing quality, market reputation or product integrity while coordinating the work of as many as (12) business critical projects simultaneously. |
| 4. Develop and implement new policies, processes, procedures and systems to ensure an efficient and effective product development. | • Drive to achieve innovation, measureable reduction in unit production cost and creative solutions to bottom line problems. A flexible approach to system design utilizing proven techniques. |
| 5. Promote cooperation and communication between the various groups within the division to ensure operational efficiency and division profitability. | • High levels of commitment by all parties and highly successful projects both domestically and overseas. |
| 6. Communicate performance metrics; evaluate performance, coach and counsel employees. Maintain harmonious employee/employer relationship | • A balanced left/right brain approach to managing employees developed over the years by mentoring from Engineering, HR and Organizational Development Executives. Proven ability to challenge other employees to achieve. |
| 7. Promote the Division, its products, services and relationships with key and potential customers | • Effective and authentic company testimony to help win new business and maintain current clients |

Please look over my professional profile which describes in further detail some examples of the results of the skills and abilities I bring to the table.

I'll check with you on June 1$^{st}$ to see about our next step unless you contact me first.

Thank you very much.

Best regards,


**Name**

1 Incl: Resume

**"CUSTOM" Works. "GENERIC" remains Unemployed**

This is how hiring managers see your boring, generic, mass-distributed resume.

This is how hiring managers see your professional profile customized to the specific requirements of their job

"Generic"
remains unemployed

"Custom"
works

*Be the **Meatball**. Don't blendinliketheforgetablefettuccini.*

## "Custom" Works. "Generic" Remains Unemployed

*"Don - 90% of job seekers are lazy and prefer to complain rather than take action. Only they can help themselves.*

*Stop worrying about them and focus on the motivated 10%. Hope that some of the 90% will see what's happening and cross over, but give your attention to the motivated 10%."*

> **Eric Castaneda.** An expert user of my D-I-Y résumé-writing system, he can get interviews whenever he wants them. What recession?

## Only 10% of you are right for my D-I-Y résumé-writing system

*"While my system isn't rocket science, it is work, something many seeking work seemingly prefer to avoid.*

*You may be one of them, which is why I say you may not be right for my system."*

> **Don Burrows.** Résumé Strategist, Workshop Leader, Author of the Amazon Kindle Best Seller **How to Get Interviews! Stop Sending Job Search Junk Mail**

# You *can* be an *IDEAL CANDIDATE* each time you apply

**FIRST STEP to be an "Ideal Candidate":** *WIN YOUR "INNER GAME"*

**Update Your Attitude** *before you* **"Update Your Résumé"**

Your **"Inner Game"** is the *"self-image"* you choose to hold in your mind. Positive or negative, that *"self-image"* determines **Your Outer Game** - the job search tools and strategies you choose to use to *"present yourself"* to recruiters and hiring managers.

Your **"Inner Game"** is your *"Self-Talk."* Positive or negative, it's your self-elevating *"Hero Story"* **or** your never-ending, downward-spiraling *"Victim Story."*

Done right, your **"Inner Game" continually reinforces your self-confidence, self-esteem, personal resiliency** and **optimism.** It sustains you through the ups-and-downs of your search for meaningful work you want to do.

**You're either winning or losing Your "Inner Game."**

*Ideal Candidates* **stand out like a** *meatball* **on a plate of spaghetti and win interviews for meaningful work they want to do**

*Generic Applicants* **blendinlikespaghetti and "settle" for whatever they can get**

**IDEAL CANDIDATES** win their **"Inner Games."** They are focused. They do not mass-distribute their *generic résumés.* Rather, **they customize their résumés and cover letters** to the specific requirements of the opportunities they seek. And they get interviews.

**GENERIC APPLICANTS** often lose their **"Inner Games."** If you're presenting yourself *generically* for work you're qualified to do and recruiters and hiring managers ignore you, and you're getting fearful because your spirit, self-confidence and self-esteem are in freefall, you're an *unfocused "generic applicant"* and **you're losing Your "Inner Game."**

SECOND STEP to be an "Ideal Candidate": *WIN YOUR "OUTER GAME"*

Once your "**Inner Game**" is strong and you've completed this *Companion Workbook* to the best of your ability, you'll be ready to **create custom résumés** and **cover letters** to **make yourself an IDEAL CANDIDATE** each time you apply.

After this *Companion Workbook,* your next step will be my D-I-Y résumé-writing book

*How to Get Interviews! Stop Sending Job Search Junk Mail*

> *If you can't get interviews for jobs you want,*
>
> *your education and experience won't matter*

## For your consideration

If you were lucky enough to get career advice from the late Zig Ziglar, legendary master sales trainer and keynote speaker, he would definitely have advised you to be *a "Meaningful Specific"* not a *"Wandering Generality."*

*"Meaningful Specifics"* never send **generic Job Search Junk Mail.** They customize their résumés and cover letters to the requirements of each opportunity they seek. Because they do that, they make themselves *"Ideal Candidates"* and they win interviews.

*"Wandering Generalities"* do the opposite. They follow the ***"Boilerplate Herd,"*** unwittingly distributing **Job Search Junk Mail** that recruiters and hiring managers ignore. *"Wandering Generalities"* take longer to get out of *"Applicant Pools"* because they prolong their unemployment.

Think of a plate of spaghetti with a meatball on top.

The *"Wandering Generalities"* are the strands of spaghetti, blendinginlikeforgettablefettucine.

The *"Meaningful Specifics"* are the MEATBALLS. They STAND OUT and are IDEAL CANDIDATES.

MEATBALLS get calls. Spaghettigetsforked.

**Be the Meatball, not the spaghetti.**

If recruiters ignore your *"Spaghetti Résumés"* and you're starting to panic, you need this **Workbook.**

Work it to be best of your ability and it will help you build your self-confidence by identifying and customizing your most **Relevant Professional Accomplishments** so you can present yourself as an **IDEAL CANDIDATE** - each time you apply.

Want interviews?

## BE THE MEATBALL.

You *can* be an **IDEAL CANDIDATE** each time you apply.

# Preface: Focus of this Workbook

If you won't quit on yourself and will complete it to the absolute best of your ability, this *Workbook* will teach you how to **win your *Inner Game.***

How sick and tired are you of applying for work you know you're qualified for and NEVER GETTING AN INTERVIEW, OR EVEN THE COURTESY OF A REJECTION LETTER?

Are you fed up enough to do something about it by applying some thought muscle and energy and trying something different?

If not, you're not right for this book, so please don't buy it.

As the police say, *"Move on. There's nothing to see here."*

But if you're ready to work to regain your self-esteem and your self-confidence, read on.

For over 35+ years, (18 of which as an in-house recruiter for all levels of positions) I've been helping job seekers, solopreneurs, freelancers and executives-in-transition win interviews for meaningful work they wanted to do. They did that by identifying and then customizing their ***representative professional accomplishments*** to the requirements of the opportunities they sought. They won interviews because they presented themselves as ***"Ideal Candidates"*** not "Generic Applicants" *each time they applied.*

Are you getting the same results with your current résumé?

## Lesson Learned

Over the years, I've learned that folks seeking meaningful work they want to do fall into one of two broad groups:

☐ **Group 1: *Generic 90%ers.*** Those who follow the ***"Boilerplate Herd"*** - *seeing and presenting themselves generically* in terms of their *"dates and duties"* résumés – nothing more than a reverse-chronological list of their work history, responsibilities / daily activities of their various jobs or gigs.

The skeletal résumés they're sending out may have worked in the last century, but not this one.

Repeating the same-old same-old and providing just the boring bare-bones minimum information, how could the sender reasonably think they'd **stand out** enough that a recruiter or hiring manager could possibly be interested enough to interview them?

They aren't, of course, so they don't.

- [ ] **Group 2: *Motivated 10%ers.*** Those who think from their **relevant professional accomplishments,** not their job chronology. They see and present themselves in terms of the problems they have faced and fixed - their relevant professional accomplishments - and the **special skills and abilities** used to achieve them.

They customize their accomplishments and skills to create targeted *custom cover letters and résumés* that *match the specific requirements of each opportunity.* Because the requirements of each position are different and they customize to the differences, they never send out the same résumé twice.

After comparing their experience with a position's requirements, if they see they cannot present themselves as an *"Ideal Candidate,"* they don't waste their time or energy applying on the off-chance they *might* get an interview.

They know what I hope you are starting to realize:

*"CUSTOM"* Works. *"GENERIC"* Remains Unemployed.

And since they only apply when they will be *"Ideal Candidates,"* they are interviewed and hired light-years faster than their *Generic* competitors.

If your job search, your optimism, and your self-confidence are all dead-in-the-water and you're playing a *losing Inner Game*, after reading those last five short paragraphs you should be trembling with excitement as you realize the implications of what you just read.

If it hasn't sunken in yet, please re-read them. And if still not, please continue reading and give yourself the benefit of not letting your ego get in the way of acknowledging you need help. Do that and you'll soon realize the benefit and the opportunity you have before you – the opportunity to exit the *"Applicant Pools"* and get onto as many *"Candidate Slates"* as you wish.

The opportunity to **win your *Inner Game*** and stop feeling ignored, squashed, or desperate.

## Traits of Generic 90%ers

I've put together a profile of the traits *Generic 90%er* share. I'm continually updating the list, so it's not all-inclusive, but is the best I have at these two minutes of time. It's not necessary to have all of them to be a *Generic 90%er*. One trait is enough. Which ones resonate personally with you?

☐ **Generic 90%ers mass-distribute Job Search Junk Mail.** Using generic reverse-chronological template résumés and hoping one or two may spark interest and an interview, they fail to differentiate themselves in a crowded market. They unintentionally and unknowingly complicate their lives, prolong their unemployment, and continue to impoverish themselves and their families.

Because of well-intended but generic advice they've accepted and acted upon, how they've chosen to see themselves and present themselves, and the job search tools they've chosen to use, *Generic 90%ers* are struggling in this economy where recruiters and hiring managers can cherry-pick from among a wealth of qualified targeted applicants and don't waste their time with **generic Job Search Junk Mail.** They *only interview* those who present themselves as *qualified for the specific position they seek.* The *Generic 90%ers* are ignored leftovers.

Without considering that their *generic mindset and generic approach may be the cause of their continued unemployment,* **Generic 90%ers** generally remain in the unemployed *"Applicant Pool"* much longer than their more focused *Motivated 10%er* competition.

☐ **Generic 90%ers often have a *"Victim"* mindset and spin their wheels endlessly *"updating their résumés."*** When the current version does not work they distribute an updated *"new* résumé" rehash of the same old ineffective résumé. When they get the same unsuccessful results, they often lament, *"There's no work. Nobody's hiring."*

That's a *"victim"* mindset, and if that mindset becomes their reality, it can be lethal, causing them to completely give up and remain permanently unemployed or only marginally employed.

The mindset is wrong.

There *is* work and people *are* getting hired – just not them.

*Yet.*

☐ ***Generic 90%ers* are just as competent and qualified as the *Motivated 10%ers*** but because they don't present themselves as effectively, they have difficulty making it onto *"candidate slates"* for meaningful work they want to do. Instead, they end up treading water in countless *"applicant pools"* or working in mediocre dead-end jobs because they couldn't get anything better.

☐ ***Generic 90%ers* often flit from one thing to another**, lacking 'stick-to-itiveness,' follow-through and personal commitment to finish what they start. They start with great optimism and enthusiasm and then take short-cuts, preferring the *"quick-and-dirty"* route rather than actually following the plan that will get them results. They ***"quit on themselves"*** and disappoint the people who took them at their word and relied on their commitments.

In the Preface to his new book ***The Motivation Manifesto***, *New York Times* Best-selling author Brendon Burchard notes that, *"Too many of us believe ourselves strong when a long gaze across our lives would sight a pattern of quitting or withdrawing too soon, often when our loved ones needed us to be strong or right when our dreams were just within reach. For convenience or the wide smile of popularity, we waffle on our word and give up what we truly believe in."*

With remarkable creativity ***Generic 90%ers*** plausibly rationalize (rational lies) their reasons for quitting on themselves and disappointing others. But that changes nothing. No matter the rationale, *"quitting"* is still quitting, *"unemployed"* is still unemployed and a *"broken promise"* to oneself or others is still a broken promise.

☐ ***Generic 90%ers* often blindly follow the *"Boilerplate Herd,"*** mostly out of fear and without much thought. They accept without question HR's self-serving and labor-saving restrictions that expedite screening of résumés. In the process they screw themselves by going *"chronologically generic."*

***Generic 90%ers*** who have unthinkingly swallowed HR's Kool-Aid® believe, act on and perpetuate the lazy, self-serving, arbitrary and damaging crap recruiters and career services staff dish out, like, *"You must organize your résumé around your job history because that's how HR wants it."* Or *"Your résumé cannot be longer than two pages because no one will read more than two pages."*

That kind of lazy *"spaghetti thinking"* is dangerous, destructive and flat-out wrong. It prolongs ***Generic 90%ers'*** job searches.

Why?

Following advice like that makes it exceptionally difficult for applicants to differentiate themselvesandstandout.Rather,theircredentialsblendinlikejustonemorestrandofspaghetti on a plate, giving recruiters no reason to select *their résumé* from the pile.

My *Motivated 10%er* readers and clients know how damaging and seriously silly *"spaghetti thinking"* is because their relevant, content-rich and customized three- or four- or five- or even six-page résumés made them STAND OUT like a MEATBALL on that plate of spaghetti and won them interviews while their generic competitors sat home staring at silent cell phones.

☐ *Generic 90%ers* **have no alternative but to present themselves generically.** Having not taken the time to complete a recent and all-inclusive personal inventory like this to identify the key accomplishments they bring to the *"World of Work,"* they have no alternative but to present themselves generically – essentially using lists of dates of employment, job activities and responsibilities. And because they blendinlikeonemorepieceofspaghettiinabowl, recruiters and hiring managers ignore them.

When you present yourself as a commonplace *"plug-and-play"* commodity, the competition is brutal and the odds of getting an interview are horrible.

☐ *Generic 90%ers* **commit Job Search Suicide**, and most companies don't even give them the courtesy of a rejection letter.

Damn! No wonder so many *Generic 90%ers* lose heart, proclaim *"Nobody's hiring"* and quit on themselves.

And you know, while it's easy to blame the companies, there's no basis for that *"victim"* mentality.

It's a Buyer's Market and employers are flooded with qualified applicants. **By wasting no time on the generic *Job Search Junk Mail* from *Generic 90%ers*,** companies are simply being practical and proactive so they can cut through the junk mail and get to the good stuff - the applicants who presented themselves as qualified candidates - faster.

If you're a *Generic 90%er,* what does that mean for you?

*It means Motivated 10%ers* **are getting your interviews and hiring is happening –** **for them.**

## It's a hell of a Catch-22

On the one hand, hopeful *Generic 90%er* applicants who follow the *"Boilerplate Herd"* queue up in HR's cattle chute and comply with the recruiters' instructions – instructions intended to expedite the recruiter's job, not enable applicants to present themselves most effectively.

And on the other hand, no matter how well-qualified they are, by complying with the company's instructions to present themselves chronologically (generically) applicants don't customize their accomplishments to the position's requirements. Being spaghetti, they provide the rope by which recruiters hang them.

A human may take *five to seven seconds* skim their superficial generic *"dates-and-duties"* reverse-chronological résumé and then consign it, unread, to a deep, dark black hole. I'm told machines scanning for key words take even less time.

## Motivated 10%ers

Here's a similar but shorter profile of *Motivated 10%ers*. It's pretty much the opposite of what you just read, with a couple of key additional points.

☐ *Motivated 10%ers* **recognize the destructive futility of going** *"victim."* They take proactive responsibility for their success. They don't blame others for their situation or wallow in it. They love key-word searches because their key-word rich custom résumés are filled with them. They don't present themselves as *"plug-and-play"* commodities, nor use cookie-cutter reverse-chronological template résumés. And they **don't quit on themselves** or *"settle"* for mediocrity.

☐ *Motivated 10%ers* **customize the three critical elements of their résumés and cover letters** (*Representative Professional Accomplishments, Special Skills* and *Abilities,* and *Objective*) to the *specific requirements of specific opportunities* and present themselves as solutions to an employer's needs – as *"Ideal Candidates."*

☐ *Motivated 10%ers* **keep the commitments they make to themselves and others**. They focus on what's important, not what's fun. Because they play a *Winning Inner Game*, they are optimistic and believe in their ability to create their own reality. They willingly invest the time and energy to customize their résumés and cover letters to the specific requirements of each opportunity they seek. They don't commit **Job Search Suicide** by mass-distributing the same generic **Job Search Junk Mail** résumé to apply for *specific positions,* hoping that *this time,* someone, *anyone,* will be interested and call them for an interview.

Rather, they only apply where it makes sense for them to apply. They do that by comparing their relevant professional accomplishments and skills with the requirement of each opportunity. If there's a match, they select and customize *only* their relevant accomplishments and skills to the position's requirements, and apply. If there's no match, they don't. They move on to other opportunities where they can be an *"Ideal Candidate."*

Their mindset is: *"If I can't be an 'Ideal Candidate,' what's the point? Why waste my time being a 'generic applicant' when I can apply elsewhere and be an* **"Ideal Candidate."'**

It saves them loads of time and the frustration that comes with being ignored because recruiters and hiring managers seldom ignore *Ideal Candidates.*

☐ *Motivated 10%ers* **share an accomplishments mindset that has nothing to do with their job level.**

*Motivated 10%ers* whom I know have used my system to win interviews and move up in the world have been sales clerks, one waitress, officers and enlisted transitioning out of the military, one carpenter, professional engineers, recent college grads looking for their first real job, self-employed individual contributors, people who have been laid off and others whose companies are reorganizing and they must reapply for their positions, managers changing careers and industries, executives, freelancers and solopreneurs.

Their unifying trait is their **accomplishments mindset** *and* how they choose to **see and present themselves** - in terms of *their accomplishments* – the problems they have faced and fixed.

They know they are so much more than a generic *"dates-and-duties"* commodity, so they never present themselves that way.

## Bottom Line

If you're a *Generic 90%er* unaccustomed to thinking about and identifying your relevant professional accomplishments and corresponding skills, at first you may find this difficult or uncomfortable and like 90% of those before you, *you may be tempted to quit on yourself.*

**Quitting on themselves** is one of the traits that keep *Generic 90%ers* unemployed. Actually, in my experience it's the main one, along with mass-distribution of generic *Job Search Junk Mail*.

Please – make *this time* the time you don't quit on yourself.

Have some faith in yourself and trust this system that has helped hundreds before you see themselves differently and win interviews – the first step to getting back to work.

Once you've completed this **Workbook** and developed the accomplishments mindset of a **Motivated 10%er,** your mind will be prepared to apply what you've learned and complete the **How to Get Interviews! Stop Sending Job Search Junk Mail** Trilogy.

At this moment, you're holding your future in your hands.

Don Burrows/Fall, 2014

# Introduction

*"Your self-image controls the results in your life. You can become the sort of person and live the sort of life you want by deciding who and what you want to be, and then acting like that person and doing the things they do. Improving your self-image is the first step towards improving your results."* Jennifer Colford. International Best Selling Author: **Managing Mothering**. <u>MomsMorningMinute.com</u>

## Update your attitude before you "update your résumé."

*"Don, I went from tongue-tied to fluently speaking, from "I don't know what I have to offer" to "This is what people gain when they work with me." The system... was challenging but so worth the effort! I am much more confident talking about my services than before."* Leona Rehm. <u>SimplyEffectiveCoaching.com</u>

If your job search is going nowhere and you're getting jumpy, panicky, depressed, or just flat-out scared, **you're losing your *Inner Game* and it is hurting you.**

**Until you start winning your *Inner Game*** simply *"updating your résumé"* yet again is a waste of time, spirit and energy.

It's the job search equivalent of rearranging deck chairs on the Titanic.

No matter how many times you *"update your résumé" and get no interviews,* like the Titanic, you're still sunk.

**Update your attitude** about ***how you choose to "see" yourself,*** how you choose to ***"present"*** *yourself* and about ***the job search tools you choose to use.***

Until you've successfully done that, you could *"update your résumé"* three times a day until Forever. You'll continue to be a *generic applicant* and you'll lose out to those who make themselves *"Ideal Candidates."* You'll blendinlikejustonemorestrandofspaghetti in a bowl and your successful search for meaningful work you want to do will continue to frustrate and elude you.

It's likely you're struggling in this niched and custom job market. You may be bewildered, angry, desperate, maybe even depressed and in panic-mode.

If so, stop. Breathe in. Breathe out. Get yourself under control.

Panic will get you nowhere, so center yourself and give yourself the gift of calm and focused thinking. Reactive flailing around and doing activity for activity's sake will only get you more of the same.

So when you get those feelings, stop. Just stop. Breathe in. Breathe out. Get centered and when you are, continue reading.

## To Win Your "Inner Game", first update your attitude, *then update your résumé*

If your *Inner Game* isn't working, neither are you. At least not in meaningful work you want.

**When you're winning your *Inner Game*,** your self-esteem and self-confidence are rock solid. Your back can be against the wall and everything is going against you, yet your core remains calm and strong. You are resourceful and believe in yourself. Your spirit remains optimistic. You are confident because you know you have marketable, relevant accomplishments and skills and you know you'll be able to market them. You see yourself and present yourself in terms of those accomplishments and skills. You don't quit on yourself. You don't give up. You have the will to **win your *Inner Game*.** And you do.

Am I describing you? Are you **winning your *Inner Game*?**

If so, see yourself as a ***Motivated 10%er.*** You probably have no immediate need of this *Companion Workbook.* You're ready for **How to Get Interviews! Stop Sending Job Search Junk Mail.**

## Critical point. Please read and understand this

**I want you to know that when you have completed this *Companion Workbook* and the How to Get Interviews! Stop Sending Job Search Junk Mail Trilogy, you will not have an updated all-purpose generic résumé to show for your time, energy and effort.**

No. Instead you will have created something much more flexible, useful and valuable:

You'll have created an expandable **Accomplishments Data Bank** filled to overflowing with **Accomplishment Statements,** little six- or seven-sentence *"stories"* detailing the relevant accomplishments of which you are most proud *and* that have most advanced your career.

You'll have created at least **two different (and for Overachievers, you'll have the opportunity to create three) Skills Data Banks** also filled to overflowing with the specific skills and abilities you used to achieve the accomplishments of which you are most proud and are most relevant to work you want to do.

And you'll have created an effective way to present the unchanging part of your résumé – what I call **"Part B"** - your work history, education, military service (if applicable), outside interests, certifications and licenses. It's the copy-and-paste second half of each of your custom résumés.

Because of the **modular format of this system** (think Legos®), your Data Banks and "Part B" are designed to grow with your career. You'll always be able to add to, update, repurpose, and customize your **Accomplishments and Skills Data Banks** to the requirements of each opportunity you seek.

*No more "updating your résumé"* because each résumé you create will be customized and unique.

When you've identified a specific opportunity you want to pursue you'll select from your **Accomplishments and Skills Data Banks only those accomplishments and skills that most closely meet the requirements of the opportunity you seek**. The accomplishment statements and skills you do not select will remain in your Data Banks until the next opportunity.

After making appropriate *"key word" edits to align your Accomplishments and Skills* with the specific position requirements, you'll present yourself as an *"Ideal Candidate"* each time you apply – where it makes sense for you to apply.

When you've followed my D-I-Y résumé-writing system as intended you'll be able to point and laugh at my tagline *(If you can't get the interview, your education and experience won't matter)* because it will no longer apply to you.

From here to the end of this *Workbook*, I estimate you are about 15 hours of actual working time away from **Updating your Attitude, starting to win your *Inner Game,* and setting the foundation to win your *Outer Game* and get interviews for meaningful work you want to do.**

When you've done that, you'll meet a very impressive new *"You."*

## So let's start with a short *"Inner Game"* baseline exercise

You've been doing a lot of thinking. Now it's time for you to do some writing.

Only twelve questions to answer. Please don't just slap down the first thing that comes to mind. Be honest. Be thoughtful and thorough. Give them the serious thought they deserve and then record your detailed and honest answers.

This is your life we're talking about, and doesn't it deserve your best effort?

There are a lot of exercises throughout the *Workbook* and because I don't want to limit what you write by providing a fixed amount of space for you to write in, I left you no space.

**My recommendation:** as you come to the *Workbook* exercises, copy the questions into either a *Companion Workbook Word document* and answer the questions electronically, or get yourself a *"Learning Journal"* you'll like to write in, copy the questions and write your answers.

In my experience, I've found that when I took the time and effort to copy the question before I answered it, I thought more deeply about the question, and my answer was more complete and beneficial to me. I believe it will be so for you as well.

I'm partial to a leather journal. Barnes & Noble has a wide selection at reasonable prices. Either way, make sure you're comfortable using it and like the feel of it so you will use it consistently. You're about to create a critical document for your life. Treat it with the respect it deserves.

Throughout the *Workbook* I'll refer to both options as your *Learning Journal* and when it's time for you to do some writing, you'll see my questions and these words:

## ~~ Time Passes ~~

# The Twelve Questions

1. Looking back from now to the start of your career, what were the critical decisions you made, did not make, *or let others make for you,* that led you to where you are now? Write about those decisions – both the good ones and the bad - and their impact on you today.

2. As a result of those decisions and other factors, do you need to make a U-turn on any of them and go in a different direction? If so, why and which ones? Be specific in how you will do that.

3. Why are you actually doing this book now? Don't settle for the immediately obvious *"to get a job."* You can get one of those at any fast food place. Really – WHY are you doing this book now?

4. Are you doing this book for yourself, or are you doing it to appease someone else? If someone else, why do you think they either gave you this book now or want you to complete this book now?

5. If your history is such that quitting on yourself and not completing this book to the best of your ability is a very real possibility, how will you get beyond what I believe is your initial enthusiasm *"now"* and maintain your motivation, self-commitment and progress through to completion?

6. If you had a career *"do-over,"* what would it be? Why?

7. What are the essential *"must-haves"* of your *"Ideal Job?"* What elements must you avoid?

8. *Yes* or *No*: Are you 100% certain you have done **everything** possible to conduct the most effective search for meaningful work? Why? Specifically, *what* have you done?

9. If **No,** what other things could you have done? Why didn't you do them?

10. While answering these questions, what additional ideas of specific short-term and longer-term actions you could take came to mind?

11. On a *Horrible-to-Wonderful* scale of 0 to 10, **where is your Inner Game right now?** Why that number?

12. What question are you thrilled / relieved I did not ask? Why? Answer it.

## ~~~ Time passes ~~

# Your Inner Game

How you play your *Inner Game* will either make you or break you.

While I suppose it's possible to have a middle ground, I don't know why you'd want to. For our purposes *you are either winning your Inner Game or you're losing it*.

Your *Inner Game* is not the big, bright *"game face"* bluff you put on for the outside world.

It's who you are, what you feel and what you say to yourself when you're scared sleepless at 2 am, with no one to impress and no one to fool.

Your *Inner Game* can go either way. It's your self-confidence, your emotional resiliency when a recruiter tells you - yet again - they hired someone else, or worse, never gets back to you. It's your sense of certainty and optimism that you'll triumph, never mind that you feel like road-kill on a hot summer day. It's your *"Self-Talk"* and your self-esteem. It's how you *"see"* yourself and *"present"* yourself – as either a winner or a loser. A Zero or a Hero.

If you're qualified for the work you seek and your search for meaningful work you want to do is going nowhere, often **your *Inner Game* is the primary thing that's keeping you unemployed, and your generic mass-distributed *"dates-and-duties"* Outer Game résumé is next.**

Why? Because if you don't feel good about *"you,"* that negative *Inner Game* vibe will shine through in the tone and content of your **Outer Game** résumés and cover letters. It's a sure bet that recruiters, hiring managers and decision-makers will pick up on that **"muh"** stuff you're putting out there.

Authentic or faking it, upbeat and confident, or desperate, fearful, maybe even depressed – it comes through in either the enthusiastic, positive tone or the spludgy *"muh"* mumble of your correspondence, and certainly in a phone screen or face-to-face interview, if you're lucky enough to get one or both.

The best way I know to **win your *Inner Game*** is to give yourself the confidence that comes from having identified and being able to speak effectively about *your relevant professional accomplishments* – the ones of which you are most proud *and* that moved your reputation, your career and your life furthest along.

If your first response to that last paragraph was, *"Yeah, right! I'm just a (fill in the blank). I have no accomplishments"* that's your *"Self-Talk"* yammering away. It is destructive. It is wrong, and it needs to change for you to move forward. We'll get to that very shortly.

Unless you're a very bad horrible person or you're dead and don't know it, you have experience, knowledge and worthwhile accomplishments for which employers will pay you money. It's all a question of how you *"see"* your accomplishments *("see" yourself = your **Inner Game**)* and the résumé tools you use to present yourself *(your **Outer Game**)*.

Don't worry if you haven't yet found your accomplishments; you will shortly. Some are hidden here in this *Workbook* and the mother lode is in ***How to Get Interviews! Stop Sending Job Search Junk Mail.*** We'll go on a treasure hunt shortly and you'll find them.

If you'll commit the time and effort to work with me here, trust the process, and most importantly, **not quit on yourself,** we're going to start identifying your **relevant professional accomplishments** so you can present yourself as an *"Ideal Candidate"* each time you apply – repeat after me: *"where-it-makes-sense-for-you-to-apply."*

This *Workbook* is like a magic mirror in which you can watch yourself grow, develop and transform from who you are now to who you want to be. But it only works if you're courageous, honest with yourself, don't quit on yourself, don't take short-cuts, and *work the process as presented.*

A quick aside. Recently a young man who has been out of work since January 2014 asked to meet with me. His résumé and answers to my questions confirmed that he is a *Generic 90%er.* I gave him an hour of coaching, guidance and explanation of my system and he bought a copy of ***Burn Your Résumé! You Need a Professional Profile.*** While he did not have the funds to retain me, I agreed to meet with him again and gave him an initial assignment to read the book cover to cover and make a list of his most relevant accomplishments and email it to me prior to our next meeting. Two weeks later he emailed me what he thought were six completed accomplishment statements. No list as I requested. Just six ineffective generic statements that varied little from what he had written in his résumé.

I gave him email feedback and returned the document. I asked if he had read the entire book to understand the process. I also asked if he had written the accomplishment essays before he wrote the accomplishment statements or if he skipped that step and just wrote the statements?

In his return email he asked for another meeting because he did not understand how to convert an *"activity"* to an *"accomplishment."* To his credit and my annoyance, he confirmed he had not read the entire book, just the chapter on accomplishment statements. He neglected to answer my second question, the one regarding writing the essays. I believe I know the answer.

I declined a second meeting, firmly suggesting he not take short-cuts and not contact me again until he had done as requested. No reply.

As I may have remarked earlier, **Generic 90%ers** often go quick-and-dirty and cause their own problems.

Think about your answers to those 12 questions. To win the interviews you need, you'll first have to come face-to-face with some of your own personal behaviors, demons and challenges, some experiences, memories or truths you may want to continue to ignore, and some questions you'd prefer to avoid or may not want to answer honestly and completely.

If you look away, close your eyes, deny or avoid the challenges, you will have quit on yourself and you won't get the prize.

Don't quit on yourself.

I struggle to understand why **10%** of those seeking work will take action, embrace and follow this system to the best of their ability, and win interviews while the other **90%,** who are just as smart, choose to procrastinate or just start flailing away without first reading the entire book they purchased and understanding the system. They start with enthusiasm and then quit on themselves, offering all sorts of reasons why they did not finish it. Life continued while they frittered away their time and many fell further into debt and some into depression.

I struggle to find just the right words to help the **90%ers** to not feel diminished by admitting they need help – which they'll find in this *Workbook*.

This *Workbook* is **a helping hand up for the *Generic 90%*** - the persistently hopeful who don't know what else to do and so continue sending out the same old generic résumés that haven't worked before. They continue hoping and betting on *"maybe this time . . . ."* And it's also for those who have thrown in the towel and given up looking for meaningful work they want to do.

They are losing their *'Inner Game'* and companies, particularly in this niched custom labor market, don't hire people who are **playing a losing *'Inner Game.'***

It's a horrible (and unnecessary) Catch-22 to be caught in, because if they'd follow the damn system, they'd learn some new and more effective personal behaviors. They could be *"Ideal Candidates"* and win interviews.

If I'm speaking to you and my words make sense, please read on and allow yourself a bit of hope, optimism, a positive spirit and the commitment to yourself and your family to see this through.

I expect you and they will be glad you did.

My hopes for this *Workbook* and for you are threefold.

FIRST, when we're done, how you see yourself will definitely have changed for the better. You'll have **Updated Your Attitude.**

SECOND, as a result of your attitude perking up, your *Inner Game* will too and then will soar.

And THIRD, when that happens, look out! You'll be ready to get serious and complete *How to Get Interviews! Stop Sending Job Search Junk Mail.* You'll fill your **Accomplishments** and **Skills Data Banks** with your greatness, and then with your *Outer Game* and your *Inner Game* in sync, you'll begin to win interviews for meaningful work you want to do.

## OK. This is the end of the Introduction.

Before moving to Chapter One, please open your *Learning Journal.*

Take a moment and capture your ideas, thoughts, feelings and what you've realized about yourself thus far.

## ~~~ Time Passes ~~~

# CHAPTER 1

# What's Your Story - "Victim" or "Response-Able"?

**Question:** Who is responsible for your career and its impact on your life?

Answer: You. No one else. Just you. It's always you.

If critical aspects of your life are not the way you want them to be, you're responsible for them and for fixing them.

No one else. Just you. It's always you.

Remember that when you go *"Victim"* and point the finger of blame at someone else, three more are pointing back at you.

**Question:** How many people do you know who have been lucky enough to work their entire career without ever being laid off?

My answer: I only know five, and I'm not one of them.

## My "Victim Story" of being laid-off

When I got laid off I could not get out from under a continual avalanche of negative emotions – primarily *scared, stupid* and *incompetent*.

I was an angry *"victim."*

I tell you that so you know I'm not just spouting a bunch of preachy pie-in-the-sky platitudes here.

I'm writing from personal, real-life experience. If you've gone *"victim,"* so have I. Maybe even more spectacularly, longer and uselessly than you.

Going *"victim"* is not what matters. What matters is whether or not you choose to live in that poisonous hole until you die, or climb out of it and get back to effectively living your life.

I know how you're feeling. And because I've done it for myself and helped others get their work life back on-track, if you'll take no short-cuts and work with my system to the best of your ability, I'm confident I can help you regain both your emotional balance and your work life.

## Our "stories"

Those of us who have experienced the crushing loss of self-esteem and self-confidence, (and often our personal and professional identity,) the pain, embarrassment and fear that comes with being told our jobs have gone away (which we often internalize as *"we failed," "we weren't good enough," or "we don't matter"*) - well, we all have our *"stories."*

If your *"stories"* are positive ones that help you **win your** *Inner Game* and contribute to your success, you're lucky. You have a solid foundation upon which to build an effective *Outer Game* of *custom résumés and targeted cover letters that make it clear why* **you are an** *"Ideal Candidate."*

However, if your *"stories"* reinforce a negative message and cause you to constantly see yourself as a *"failure"* or *"victim,"* or *"mediocre,"* or *"not enough,"* your *"stories"* and the meanings you attach to them are keeping you stuck.

***And unless we're careful it is very easy, inviting and enticing*** to get caught up in them to the point that our *"stories"* become our *"realities."*

That needs to change. Now. Because the longer you wait, the harder it will be. Like thrashing around in quick sand. Do it long enough and pretty soon you get sucked under and disappear.

*Blup.*

All that drama makes you miserable, pushes away everyone who loves you, and ruins your life.

## Why I've earned the right to advise you

I've gone through what you are going through. I survived. I thrived. I know how you feel. And I know how to help.

When I got laid off, I didn't know any better and repeatedly asked myself lots of normal, understandable, panicky, and ultimately useless *"victim"* questions that kept me struggling in the quick sand of *"victim"* mode.

Questions like *"Why me?" "What did I do wrong?" "Will anyone ever hire me again?" "OMG! What am I going to do?" "Who will help me?" "What do I tell people?" "They told me I was being laid off, but was I really fired?" "What'll I do if I run out of money before I find another job?"* And over and over again, **"Why me? I'm a good person. What did I do wrong?"**

Do any of those sound familiar?

Along with the *"victim"* questions come the *"victim"* emotions.

I've felt many of the same out-of-control-rip-your-guts-out-roller-coaster emotions I know you have.

Mine were *shock, doubt, anger, frustration, embarrassment, worry, fear, panic, terror and rage.*

A lot of *rage.* For years. Decades, actually.

In one particularly memorable moment of mind-numbing rage I released some of it for a moment by punching a solid oak door. I fractured my hand. The rage went away for an instant and then came roaring back, along with the pain.

News flash: solid oak doors always win. Hands down. (Pun intended.)

I spent years of self-induced pain bumbling around in what I now think of as *"Victim Valley."* Intermittently for years my *"Self-Talk"* was such that I was not always the honorable, decent, caring man I had always told myself I was, prided myself on being, and tried to be.

I tell you all that to make this point: Having found my way out of *"Victim Valley"* sane and successful, I've earned the right to be your guide.

Time for a little cathartic *"Show-and-Tell."* I know of no more appropriate and uselessly pathetic *"Victim Story"* than my own so I'm going to make an example of myself in hopes you'll learn from my mistakes.

I bet you have a *"story"* of your own, so be thinking about it because in a few minutes I'm going to offer you an opportunity I never thought about and I don't recall anyone ever suggesting to me.

I'm going to invite you to write your *"Victim Story"*, in detail, so you can acknowledge it and then blow it away, once-and-for-all.

## My "Victim" Story, or *"How to Play a 20-Year Losing 'Inner Game' "*

Summer, 1988 was my critical time.

The divorce I requested to end my marriage of 15 years was finalized

The judge. (*Ahhh. The judge.*)

> Turns out he and my ex knew each other from the church they both attended. Mere moments before he ~~passed sentence~~ *sorry, rendered his decision,* he dropped that little bombshell on my attorney and me. His Honor sanctimoniously intoned that when we all met for the first time months before neither he nor my ex saw any reason to disclose that information, nor for him to recuse himself, because he was certain he could be *"impartial."* (*If so, why tell us now, moments before rendering his decision, but not when we first met and my attorney could have filed for a different and truly impartial judge? Seems CYA and fishy, doesn't it?*)

> *"Impartial's"* ass! I labored long and hard to fill out my financials honestly and accurately - down to the penny. When it was time for *"Financial Show and Tell,"* my ex said she hadn't had time to finish hers. His (*"Impartial"*) Honor told her she didn't need to do them.

> Repeat after me: *"Judicial Screw Job!"*

> His *"impartial"* decision: Since we were married for 15 years, I got to pay her alimony for 15 years.

> For openers, he *impartially* set the figure at $1,600 a month. (No clue how he determined that was a fair amount based on her needs because as I said, she never submitted her financials.)

> I'll move on. Some of the $1,600 a month was CS (child support) and that was fine, but most was alimony and tuition for her Master's degree.

> People with more experience than I on Alimony Road told me later that the award was extreme in the extreme and that I got screwed. Now armed with external validation, I felt entitled, even compelled, to go *"victim"* and obsessed on the unfairness of it all. For years – that's y-e-a-r-s – I never missed an opportunity to tell my *"victim"* story. I lost count of the number of women who said they wished His Honor had been *their* judge.

If he had recused himself rather than hear the case, we would have had a different judge and things may have turned out differently. If only . . .

I got sympathy and it felt good to (endlessly) tell my *"poor me pity party victim story."*

But of course all that did was keep my head, my heart, and my spirit glued to my anger, and changed nothing.

Except that without my being aware of it, my anger affected me in ways I have only recently begun to realize . . .

As I shut down my marriage, I also:

1.  Managed the Human Resources shut-down of my employer's Area headquarters. I laid off 90 colleagues, and to insulate myself from what was going on at home, immersed myself in running an in-house outplacement center for them. My efforts were the direct reason all 90 found new jobs equal to or better than the ones they lost

2.  Researched, wrote and final-typed 95% of a book - an original Area Study of Paraguay for the Army Reserves, and

3.  Packed up my half of our household goods and the company relocated me from Miami to Philadelphia.

While that $1,600/month took a huge bite out of my paycheck in Philadelphia, where the cost-of-living was more than in Miami, (a fact that was of absolutely no interest to His Honor), mad as hell, I never missed a payment.

I tell you all that to set the emotional stage for this:

In May, 1990, I was recruited and accepted a position back in South Florida, a part of the world I never liked but went back to so I could be near my two school-age children.

As I adjusted to my new life in Philadelphia and then in South Florida, my emotions began to stabilize and my **Inner Game** began to improve.

Seven months into my new job, my new employer announced plans to shut down my location to *"refocus on our core competencies."* I was one of 130 people on the street.

Suddenly all I could think about was that $1,600-a-month axe ready to fall on my neck. With the layoff, my **Inner Game** and my fragile belief that my life was getting back on-track became a toxic train wreck. I know I looked at the world through always-angry *"victim"* eyes.

$1,600 a month, and I assure you His Honor didn't give a damn that I had no job. He wanted to make sure his church friend got her money.

I so wanted to vent my anger and tell the world my *"victim"* story that I bought the website **JudicialScrewings.com** intending of create a forum for other *"victims"* to tell their judicial *"victim"* horror stories and hammer unethically biased judges like mine. (I didn't build it; last I checked, it's still available, so if you want it, have at it.)

Looking back, I realize that even though I requested the divorce and got what I wanted, my sense of self-worth and self-esteem was shaky. **I was playing a losing *Inner Game,* and what really mattered was that I didn't know it.**

Maybe my new employer picked up on that vibe, and maybe I caused my own layoff.

My anger at what my attorney said was collusion between the judge and my ex was a 24/7 white-hot flame, punctuated by outbursts of rage. I never missed an opportunity to fan that flame while I lived in Philadelphia, and with the move back to South Florida – what to me was the scene of the crime – moment-to-moment I poured gasoline on it. Self-immolation.

As the kids got older, the CS payments stopped and I got some breathing room. The alimony continued and with each check I wrote, the anger flared up. It took about ten years – that's *t-e-n* years - into the 15 before I *realized*, and then *accepted*, and finally really *believed*, that with each check I wrote I should be that much happier since I was one check closer to the final check.

Logically I always *knew* that, but damned if I *felt* it.

Ten years of useless, pointless, self-inflicted pain rehashing a never-ending story of *"victim"* anger.

The longer I held on to my *"story"* the more embedded it became and the more it consumed me, like cancer.

And here's the kicker: I thought that when I finished the obligation in 2003, all the anger and sense of *"victim"* would suddenly dissipate. Poof!

Noooo. Over 15 years I had built a fortress around my anger. I dug my nails into it and hung on to it for years after the obligation ended. It was part of who I was, even after I remarried.

It wasn't until August 30, 2011 that I experienced an internal and very physical sensation of coming *"unstuck,"* what psychotherapist Dr. Eugene Gendlin, Ph.D. calls a *"Felt Shift"* in his book **Focusing.** Why then? I don't know. I guess I had been processing what he refers to as *"all of that"* for years and something just clicked in my subconscious. And in an instant, the knot of anger I'd been holding for over two decades simply dissolved.

Immediately I wrote a letter to my ex. I said everything I needed to say. The words just poured out. It was a long letter. That evening at dusk I used sage to purify myself, the letter and the fire pit in my back yard.

I lit what I called *a "Forgiveness Fire,"* and feeling as much forgiveness and gratitude as I could for the *"felt shift"* and all it encompassed, I slowly and thoughtfully read by firelight and then burned each page of the letter, releasing into the sky the last of my residual anger, bitter memories and other accumulated damaging emotions.

I burned to ash the entire contents of the fire pit, except this one stick that I used to stir the fire.

Photo by Don Burrows

The stick lives on a shelf in front of my desk - a tangible reminder of successfully **Updating my Attitude, Winning my *Inner Game*** and achieving the positive mindset I intend to maintain.

So that's my *"story"* and I'm no longer stickin' to it.

## Are you still "stuck" in your "Story"?

If so," my guess is that it is gnawing away at you like mine was at me.

Because I've experienced first-hand the healing power of seeing my own words appear before my eyes both on-screen and on paper, I want you to have that opportunity.

Please follow the instructions. Take as much time as you need to get your *"story"* down in your *Learning Journal.*

## Instructions:

What's your *"story?"* Write it out. All of it. Leave nothing out. Purge it from your system.

Don't tighten up or edit your thoughts. Just let it flow. Don't edit your words because there's no reason for you to share what you write with anyone.

After you've finished dumping your core, read what you wrote and take another dump. Be sure you've got it all out.

After you've finished, please answer the questions that follow, **then put this aside and take a 24-hour break.**

**Then,** after your 24-hour break, reread what you wrote. Don't edit a single word. Just read. If you left out something important, add it. When you're certain you have it all down, leave it alone and continue with the *Workbook*.

## Please write your "story"

## ~~ Time passes ~~

## Questions about what you just wrote

1.   How was that experience?  Fun? Painful? Easy? Difficult? Boring? Freeing? Something else? What?

2.   What new or forgotten things did you learn, realize or recall about yourself?

3.   In just one word, how would you describe how you are feeling right now? Why that word?

**And now the three most important questions for this exercise:**

4.   Do you want to hang on to your *"story,"* or do you want to drop it like a hot slap and get on with your life?

5.   If you want to hang on to it, why? What good is it doing you? Really. *What good?*

6.   If you've decided to drop it, first of all GOOD FOR YOU! Now, what will you replace it with? Start laying it out now and keep refining it throughout the *Workbook* in your *Learning Journal.* We will come back to it in the **In Closing** section.

## ~~ Time Passes ~~

OK. You've written your *"story"* and you've answered the questions.

You've done enough *Workbook* work for the next 24 hours.

Time for a break. Don't read any more of this book.

Think some about what you wrote, but mostly . . .

Go out and play. Have a PBJ. And don't forget to come back. . . .

## 24 hours later. . . All right. You had an experience yesterday

I'm choosing to believe you wrote thoroughly and honestly, so there's no need to revise or revisit it ever again because it resides in your head and your heart, where over time it will fade to nothing more than a tiny whisper of memory.

By the end of the *Workbook*, I'll have done my best to help you dissolve the power of your *"Victim story"* and release it, substituting instead your heightened awareness of your relevant professional accomplishments.

While you were off yesterday, I'm sure you thought about what you wrote. With the distance of a day, please answer these questions:

1. After 24 hours, what were your ideas, thoughts and feelings since you finished writing your *"victim story?"*

2. If you had any flashes of insight or big *ah-ha's,* what were they? Details, please.

3. Is your *"victim story"* still valid and working for you? If *yes, no,* or *partially,* please describe.

4. If you think maybe it's time to stop seeing yourself as a *"victim"* and distance yourself from your *"story"* what are your thoughts about how you might do that? How would you *"reframe"* it or *"rewrite"* or *"reject"* it into a new *"story"* that serves you?

5. Any thoughts on how you would like to symbolically say good-bye to your old *"story"*?

6. Free play. What else do you want to write down – like maybe thoughts about accomplishments from your new *"story"* that make you proud?

## ~~ Time Passes ~~

And now it's on to Chapter 2. You do know you're talking to yourself – right?

# CHAPTER 2

# Your "Self-Talk"

Your *"Self-Talk"* is all that chatter always going on inside your head.

It can be positive and build you up, or it can be negative and rip you to shreds.

My negative *"Self-Talk"* was caused by *"my stuff"* – just as yours is caused by *"your stuff."* Mine was fear and lack of self-esteem based on why felt I didn't deserve the good things I wanted.

Maybe the same for you? Maybe not? I don't know. It was just a question. Make notes in your *Learning Journal* if you wish.

## ~~ Time Passes ~~

I live north of Seattle. In 2014 our Seattle Seahawks won the Super Bowl under the inspired leadership of our Quarterback Russell Wilson. I don't know anyone who has mastered **Self-Talk and Preparation** as well as he has. You can Google *"Russell Wilson and Self Talk"* to read interesting posts about how he prepares himself. One post I particularly like is *"The separation is in the preparation."*

Whether or not you're a football fan, I hope you took advantage of my little side-trip.

Here's a complimentary *Inner Game* perspective.

**John Maxwell in his <u>How Successful People Think Workbook</u> quotes Denis Waitley, author of <u>The Psychology of Winning</u> as saying: *"The winners in life think constantly in terms of 'I can, I will and I am.' Losers, on the other hand, concentrate their waking thoughts on what they should have done, or what they don't do." If you believe you can't do something, then it doesn't matter how hard you try, because you've already lost. If you believe you can do something, you have already won much of the battle."***

**Among others, one of the most damaging aspects about simultaneously playing a losing *Inner Game* and *playing the "victim"* is that you're living an energy-sucking debilitating contradiction and you probably don't know it.**

When I was in lay-off mode, unknowingly defining myself through my *"victim-ness"* and losing my **Inner Game,** I would have resisted, really pushed back hard, if anyone had ever challenged me, told me I was acting like a *"victim"* and that the *"Pity-Party Drama Queen"* thing was really old and unattractive.

We don't know what we don't know.

## My *"Self-Talk"* went something like this:

*"Damn judge."*

*"I'm 44 years old and here I am laid off. I'm almost 50. No one's going to want to hire me."*

*"Only screw-ups get laid off. Companies keep their good performers. I thought I was a good performer and here I am – laid-off. So I'm a screw-up."*

*"I am mega-screwed. I was a VPHR for seven months and an HR Director for ten years. I'm in a damn Catch-22 – not enough time-in-grade to say I'm an experienced VPHR, and having been a VP no recruiter will touch me because they'll think I don't want to take a back-step to Director."*

*"What'll I do if my savings run out before I find work? Go live with my parents and be their 44 year old failure son living in their guest bedroom?"*

*"How do I take care of my kids? They'll think their Dad is a failure, and they'll be right."*

*"And then there's all that crap my ex is yapping around about me to my relatives and our former friends. Ha! Some friends!"*

*"And then there's the $1,600 a month alimony and CS. And my kids tell me she spends most of my money on herself."*

*"I even tried to go back on active duty for Desert Storm and not even the Army wanted me. I suck."*

Can you see how damaging that *"Self-Talk"* was when it ran free 24/7 through my head, my heart and my subconscious?

It was all fear-based crap. When I really let myself get caught up in it, it continually clogged my mind, like a swirling clogged toilet that won't flush.

That toxic waste is over 20 years in the past, and I can still feel it scratching in my bones. Gone, but not forgotten.

Fortunately, today I acknowledge it as just part of *"who I was"* and it no longer determines *"who I am."*

Please read that last sentence again. It's vital to me, and if you're trying to find a way out of *"Victim Valley"* it should be for you as well.

After being laid off, over a six-month period I followed the outplacement firm's template résumé process, sent out over two hundred résumés, went on three interviews and got no takers.

Big surprise.

Twenty-four/seven, my *"Swirling Self-Talk"* was my constant companion. I must have been a real delight.

It was only after one of those three interviews that a senior VPHR told me why he wouldn't hire me:

He said his boss would fire him and promote me into his position.

It took me a few days to get over my anger and realize the gift he had given me. I had an epiphany and began to see myself and present myself differently.

I decided that if that if he saw me as senior VPHR material, I should see myself that way as well – (playing a new and more effective **Inner Game.**)

Hindsight being 20/20, I now see that the outplacement company's generic approach had me sending out hundreds of pieces of what I now call **Job Search Junk Mail**, garbage that all but three companies rightfully trashed.

On-the-spot, I changed both **my *Inner* and *Outer Games*.**

I stopped following the outplacement company's generic job search guidance.

I got very clear on my **Relevant Professional Accomplishments**, and as I did, I felt a positive surge in my self-confidence and self-esteem.

I redid my *Outer Game* - cover letter and résumé to showcase **my favorite Representative Professional Accomplishments and related skills with the intention of creating a job for myself that contained *only* the things I liked to do and had been successful doing.** I devised and implemented a new search strategy and it worked.

Almost immediately I began to get interviews and within about five weeks was hired.

After you've completed this *Workbook,* when your *"Self-Talk"* is again on solid ground and your **Inner Game** is ready, you'll find the specific strategies I used to turn my **Outer Game** around in **How to Get Interviews! Stop Sending Job Search Junk Mail.**

But right now, it's time for you to bring your *"Self-Talk"* up into the light-of-day.

## So what do you say? What's your "Self-Talk"?

I shared a bunch of my *"Self-Talk"* with you a minute ago.

Your turn. *Learning Journal,* please. Don't edit. What's the first thing that comes into your mind? Write it down and then keep writing. When you think you're done, pause, then write some more.

Like your *"victim"* story – please dump your core. Get it all out.

## ~~ Time passes. ~~

If you did a thorough job, I think it likely you are feeling some form of negativity, and maybe are pissed at me for asking you to dredge up all that garbage.

If so, GOOD! That means you've engaged with the process.

While the emotions are powerful and can leave you drained, they are, after all, only emotions.

You control them, not the other way around. Use your head and your heart and move through them.

Like the lyric from the song from Disney's **Frozen,** *"I'm never going back / The past is in the past."*

Let it go. Let it all go.

If you didn't *"let it go,"* please stop reading and repeat the exercise.

## The reason I asked you to do that is because we generally don't know what we don't know.

My guess is that you've never taken the time, or perhaps have purposely avoided the pain of actually surfacing that stuff, to write it all down so you can blow it away.

When I was in the middle of it, I was completely unaware that I was victimizing myself, nor did I ever think about writing down my *"story"* so I could face it and then burn it up. As a result, for years I was a swirling toilet and all my crap just kept bubbling up and now and again splattered on others.

In other words, I didn't know what I didn't know. Like tough love, you gotta deal with it before you can flush it out of your system and get healthy.

So by now you know the drill. My *Self-Talk* questions are these:

1.  Now what? What are you going to do with, and about, *"all that"*?  Really. Specifics, please.

2.  Read and really think about each bullet point of your *"Self-Talk."* Which one is THE BIGGIE, the one that hurts you the most, the one that if you could blow it up and make it disappear forever, it would go a long way toward clearing up several others? Write out THE BIGGIE. Elaborate on it, in detail.

3.  If you resolved THE BIGGIE, what others would be taken care of as well?  Don't force it, but include all you can.

## ~~ Time Passes ~~

## Reprogramming your subconscious mind

I know for a fact that, for better or worse, my *"Self-Talk"* is always running in my subconscious mind. And yours is too, whether or not you're aware of it.

I'm an enthusiastic fan of Napoleon Hill. He wrote several books, including Think and Grow Rich and Law of Success. If you haven't read them, I urge you to do both you and your **Inner Game** a favor and fix that. Now. And if you'd prefer to watch and listen rather than read, you'll find videos on YouTube of him reading both books.

Napoleon's rags-to-riches *"story"* is important for us both.

In 1908, the aging billionaire steel giant Andrew Carnegie, (the Bill Gates of his day,) selected young Napoleon (age 25) to personally meet with and document the success strategies and lessons of the 500 richest men and women of that era, before they died and the world lost their knowledge.

Carnegie opened his address book of the shakers-and-movers of the day, including Thomas Edison and Henry Ford, and introduced Napoleon to all of them. He estimated it would take Napoleon 20 years to complete the project. He covered all his business expenses, and paid him not one thin dime, figuring Napoleon would earn as he learned.

**He did not have an easy time of it and his biography (<u>A Lifetime of Riches</u>) is interesting. It's available on Amazon.**

**Knowing the project would be difficult, Carn**egie gave Napoleon an affirmation to condition his subconscious mind so he would believe in himself and be able to complete the assignment.

Please stop reading and Google: *PowerAffirmations.com/Napoleon Hill's first affirmation given to him by Andrew Carnegie.* I promise it will be time well-spent.

## ~~ Time passes.~~

I hope you did as I asked, read the story and the affirmation, and thought about how you can apply the lesson to your life. If you skipped it, **please go back and read it** and the story behind it.

I'll wait.

Quoting from <u>www.PowerAffirmations.com</u>, this is the affirmation Andrew Carnegie gave to Napoleon Hill: *"**Andrew Carnegie, I'm not only going to equal your achievements in life, but I'm going to challenge you at the post and pass you at the grandstand.**"*

That affirmation is a grand example of positive *"Self-Talk,"* and I'm sure you read Napoleon's initial negative reaction.

Had Carnegie not given him the basis for his new *"Self-Talk,"* and had Napoleon gone **Generic 90%er** and not kept his promise to himself to use it, it seems reasonable that **Napoleon Hill would have started and then quit on himself,** and the world would be the poorer.

## For you: Two important questions and one thing to really think about

**Question:** When you start a big project, are you confident you'll be able to complete it, or do you worry and immediately go to a place of self-doubt? *Yes* or *No*?

**Question:** When someone gives you a compliment, do you say *"thank you!"* with genuine enthusiasm, or do you deflect, deny, dismiss, downplay or disregard it? *Yes* or *No*?

If you answered *"Yes"* to either or both, please i-m-m-e-d-i-a-t-e-l-y begin to reprogram your subconscious mind with something more enabling and empowering.

Something like a variation of Carnegie's affirmation, or this: *"I have many accomplishments. Companies need and will pay me well for what I can do."* You'll find others at www. PositiveDailyAffirmations.com.

Positive affirmations like these lead to *"empowering beliefs"* and positive *"Self-Talk."*

**STOP and THINK** how your life would be if *at your core* you *really* believed in yourself and fed yourself a continual diet of positive *"Self-Talk"* or *"empowering beliefs"*?

## REALLY! RIGHT NOW. DON'T JUST GO ON CRUISE-CONTROL AND KEEP READING. STOP AND THINK WHAT BELIEVING THEM WOULD MEAN TO YOU.

Before you continue, capture those thoughts and feelings.

## ~~ Time passes ~~

You did stop and write down your thoughts, right?

Good! You're getting the hang of this *Motivated 10%er* stuff!

As they say, *"How you do anything is how you do everything."*

To **Update your Attitude** and **Win your *Inner Game***, you can, and you must, reprogram your subconscious with new beliefs that serve you.

You read how Carnegie helped Napoleon Hill.

Here's another method I know from experience works, if you're willing to work to make it work.

## *"Self-Talk"*: From Damaging to Helpful

*First:* Get a Sharpie in your favorite color

*Second:* Put a very visible half-inch diameter dot on whichever hand and knuckle you wish. My favorite is the base of my left thumb. Why there? No clue. Where's yours?

*Third:* Assign a meaning (an affirmation) to the dot. For our purposes now, the dot means *"I have knowledge and accomplishments that a company needs and will gladly pay for."* If you prefer, write your own meaning

*Fourth:* Each time you look at that dot, say the affirmation with conviction. Say it like you believe it. Say it to yourself. Say it out loud. Say it over and over while you're awake

*Fifth:* Invite your subconscious to take the words in and make them part of your new *"Self-Talk"* and your belief system. As you fall asleep, concentrate on the dot. Rub it and repeat your affirmation

*Sixth:* Reapply the dot when it washes off. Keep it clearly visible. Once your subconscious mind gets used to it, you won't be aware of it but as your eyes see the dot as your hand moves or gestures, it will subconsciously reinforce the meaning

*Seventh:* Do this without fail for one month and watch how your attitude changes.

This is not New Age argle-bargle. Like Andrew Carnegie's affirmation, it works if you give your word to yourself, commit to it, choose to believe it works, and if you'll work to make it work.

Do it! Really - what have you got to lose? Is your life going so great that trying this for a month would screw it up?

And do you really care what some non-entity stuck in their own mental and emotional traffic jam says or thinks about the dot?

Along with the dot, I suggest you enlist the help of someone who cares about you.

If someone you trust loves you and cares about you and is willing to reinforce their love with straight talk and support, count yourself fortunate, thank them and let them. They have your best interest at heart and you're lucky to have their help.

And be aware that they're demonstrating love and significant courage by putting themselves on the line by possibly telling you things you won't want to hear, but that you need to hear.

Set up whatever personal ground rules or boundaries you need to and then get busy.

I tell you now: this won't be a one-shot deal. Like Napoleon Hill, you'll have to work it to make it work. So adopt **Motivated 10%er** behavior and apply focused intention and practice. Make it work.

**So. With all that under your belt, please go back to each of your negative pieces of "Self-Talk" and rewrite each so it is positive.**

Let me give you an example using my first one.

**Negative:** *"I'm 44 years old and here I'm laid off. No one's going to want to hire me."*

**Positive:** *"What an opportunity! Out of a job I didn't much like, with some severance, and a chance to make a new life!"*

Lemons into lemonade.

*Learning Journal:*

## ~~ Time Passes ~

Hang on tight to what you write and make sure you can find it when you need to.

YOUR ASSIGNMENT: when you first wake up, get in front of your mirror and read out loud the positive *"Self-Talk"* affirmation that resonates most strongly with you. Read it with passion. Like you believe it. Then go have you first cup of coffee. Then repeat it throughout the day. Repeat at bedtime. Please do this for a month. You will be a very different person and you may influence the world.

Like Napoleon Hill.

# CHAPTER 3

# Cure for Being "Victim": The Accomplishments of Which You Are Most Proud

**STRAIGHT TALK:** You cannot *"Update Your Attitude"* or **Win Your** *Inner Game* when you see yourself as the *"victim."* The anger will eat you up inside, like cancer.

I'm uncomfortable, for me and for you, for linking *"victim"* and *"cancer."* But unfortunately I've seen them both first-hand, and to me the comparison is both powerful and accurate.

When you *"see"* yourself differently and more positively, it's like chemo or holistic treatments for cancer. The bad stuff starts to dissolve, shrivel up and disappear.

You'll start to *"Update Your Attitude"* and **Win Your** *Inner Game*.

The way you're going to do that is by getting clear on, acknowledging, and taking pride in your **relevant accomplishments**, both personal and professional, the ones that advanced your self-confidence, your self-esteem, your reputation, your career and your life.

Even though I went *"victim"* for two decades, in retrospect I realize I had two mega-accomplishments that took me a while to realize and acknowledge:

1.  For 15 years, month in and month out, *"I NEVER missed a payment."* Over those 15 years, I wonder how many hundreds or thousands of men did and were arrested for non-payment?

2.  *"With the help of friends and family I came out of a difficult situation better than when I went in."* I know people who did not. And you probably do as well.

Those are two exceptionally pivotal personal accomplishments that had a profound impact on my professional life.

I'm proud of these two. I claim them, and I have built a new life upon them. They reflect positively on my character, and since you know how rabidly committed I was to my anger and how determined I was to perpetuating my own *"pity-party,"* I invite you to imagine *the mindset shift* that happened for those two accomplishments to become real.

The sooner I was able to stop seeing myself as a *"victim"* and instead see myself positively, as a man who fulfilled his obligations, whether he actively sought them out or they were forced on him, whether he agreed with them or not, the sooner I was able to get *my mindset* and my *"Inner Game"* refocused *away* from the infinite loop of blame and the toxic rubble of the past and focus on a positive future, *one that I had both the responsibility and the opportunity to create.*

If you're wandering in *"Victim Valley"* and wallowing in your *"story"* please begin thinking about your major personal and professional accomplishments.

## The Lesson

When I **intentionally** acknowledged and accepted the reality that $1,600 a month was the initial price I had to pay to get what I wanted, **I finally redefined my reality** and took pride in meeting the legal and financial obligation. Instead of angrily cursing each check I wrote, I began to focus on the future and getting one step closer to having the end in sight.

I came to terms with my reality and dropped **the *"poor-me-pity-party "Victim" mindset.***

While I can't prove it, I believe that doing so enabled my 2011 *"felt shift"* from *"Victim"* to *"Response-Able"* and at that point I began to really win my *Inner Game.*

How nice it would have been to have put all this together sometime during those 15 years.

Oh well.

According to motivational speaker Richard Santana (aka Mr. Chocolate – on YouTube) *"Stupid people learn from their own mistakes. Smart people learn from the mistakes of others."*

Please learn from my mistakes.

**And maybe as you go through the *Workbook* it might be helpful to also read Dr. Gendlin's book (*Focusing*)?**

Enough about my stuff.

It's time for you to think and write about your *Inner Game,* and the accomplishments of which you are most proud.

**Question:**

I've heaped a lot on you. *How are you feeling right now?*

*Learning Journal.* Please take a moment and answer that question.

## ~~Time Passes ~~

And start thinking about the accomplishments of which you are most proud.

We'll get to them in Chapter 5, but to get there we have to go through Chapter 4.

Which do you prefer – the meatball or the spaghetti?

# CHAPTER 4

# "Custom" Works. "Generic" Remains Unemployed

This is how hiring managers see your boring, generic, mass-distributed resume.

"Generic" remains unemployed

"Custom" works

This is how hiring managers see your professional profile customized to the specific requirements of their job

*Be the **Meatball**. Don't blendinliketheforgetablefettuccini.*

Please memorize the picture and the captions.

They are the key to your future success for meaningful work you want to do.

## Do you really believe *"There's no work! Nobody's hiring!"*?

As a Job Seeker, Freelancer, Executive-in-Transition or Solopreneur – if you do, that has to be incredibly difficult, frustrating and scary: looking for work **and** believing there is no work and no one is hiring.

If that's what you truly believe **and yet you keep trying**, that makes you a hero in my book. And since this *is* my book, you are deserves a ton of credit for your heroic perseverance. You really do.

**STRAIGHT TALK:** Keep that *"perseverance"* point in mind. In your *Learning Journal* please label a page **"MY TRAITS, SPECIAL SKILLS AND ABILITIES."**

## Your Traits, Special Skills and Abilities

*Learning Journal.*

Make *"Perseverance"* your first entry and keep adding to the list as we go along.

As a matter of fact, stop for a bit and let your mind identify other **traits, skills and abilities** you *know* you have.

Start that list right now, and keep adding to it throughout the *Workbook*.

## ~~~Time Passes~~~

The worthwhile companies you want to work for value and reward employees with perseverance.

Therefore, I want you to start thinking of yourself in terms of that trait and other important **traits, skills and abilities** you possess that employers value.

Because this is critical stuff, I want you to *feel those traits, skills and abilities of yours* – *not just think about them* at an intellectual level – but rather *feel them deep in your bones*.

## So back to my question: "Do you really believe there's no work? Nobody's hiring"?

What do you think? Take some time and write down your thoughts to both questions. Not from your "They-make-these-seats-too-damn-small" *"Victim Story"* but rather from the perspective of being *"Response-Able"* and what you're learning about yourself.

*Learning Journal.*

1.    True, or not? Why, or why not?

2.    Or is the truth really that *"there's no work **for me** and no one's hiring **me?**"*

3.    And if we add the word, *"YET!"* – now what do you think?

## ~~~Time Passes~~~

If you're a *Generic 90%er* contending with all the stress brought on by your *"victim story"* and your negative *"Self-Talk"* while doing the best you know how to find meaningful work you want to do and getting nowhere, it makes sense if you hold the *"limiting beliefs"* that *there's no work* and *nobody's hiring*.

And it makes it damn near impossible to go out there and give it your best effort if you believe you're wasting your time. (The Army has a more colorful term for *"wasting your time"* and if you know it and remember how that frustration felt, recall it now and use it to power through to the positive side.)

Because if in spite of that you keep plugging away, I say again, you are a *"persistent hero."*

Give yourself credit. Take a minute and roll that thought around in your head and your heart.

*"Persistent hero."*

*"Persistent hero."*

So your tongue gets used to saying it and your subconscious gets used to believing it, say it out loud a bunch of times now and throughout the day, over the next month:

*"I'm a persistent hero."*

How does that feel? How does that sound?

Pull a Napoleon Hill. Honor your commitment to yourself and keep doing it. The more you do, the better it will sound and feel. And you'll like it and become it, more and more.

## "Update Your Attitude" with Positive *"Self-Talk"* and Positive Affirmations.

Everything we're doing here is intended to help you *"reframe"* how you *"see"* yourself – all to help you **Update your Attitude** so you can *play a stronger and more confident Inner Game.*

Back to the two questions of *no work* and *nobody's hiring.*

*Motivated 10%ers* whose education and experience are similar to yours and who are playing **strong Inner and Outer Games** would disagree with you.

There *is* work and people *are* getting hired. They know that's true because *they are getting interviews* and *many are getting hired.*

Aside from winning their **Inner Games** and not seeing themselves as *"victims,"* one of the main differences between **Generic 90%ers** who list their job duties, responsibilities and daily activities, and **Motivated 10%ers** is they **have a clear sense of their relevant accomplishments and skills**, know they have worth in the job market, and know how to customize that information to the requirements of the opportunities they seek.

*Motivated 10%er Meatballs* do not use generic résumés that makethemblendinlikejustone morepieceofspaghettiinthebowl. They customize their résumés and cover letters to the requirements of each opportunity they seek. They make themselves *"Ideal Candidates,"* not generic applicants.

I may have mentioned that earlier.

And this:

**"Custom"** Works. **"Generic"** Remains Unemployed.

There *is* work (just not for you.) People *are* getting hired (just not you.)

**YET.**

**Remember:** If you can't get interviews for work you want, your education and experience won't matter.

And **"CUSTOM"** works. **"GENERIC"** remains unemployed.

And **you can be an "Ideal Candidate"** each time you apply.

If you continue sending out *the same generic résumés* for positions with *different requirements* you will either remain unemployed longer (maybe forever) or prolong your unemployment.

I know I'm hammering these points and if you find the repetition annoying, your reaction is typical of a *Generic 90%er* who prefers to gloss over critical points and move on to the next critical point they'll gloss over, rather than focusing, acknowledging, internalizing, fixing and building upon them.

Interestingly, *Motivated 10%ers* get it and appreciate the repetition's reinforcement because they recognize the truth of it.

*Generic 90%ers*, on the other hand, say they *"get it"* but really don't, because they have not yet developed enough personal discipline to master the concept and then put it into practice.

Master sales trainer and speaker Zig Ziglar said, *"Repetition is the mother of learning."*

Are you learning?

I wonder. I hope. Are you aware of how much you have grown and we are over half-way through the book?

**If you're still with me and haven't blown me off by quitting on yourself** because I keep reiterating critical concepts, how about giving me a little more time?

With your future success as the prize, will it make your head explode if you give me a little bit more of your patience, energy, curiosity and open-minded attention?

If you've been diligent with the exercises thus far, I believe we've laid the foundation for you to begin to fly.

You *can* be an *"IDEAL CANDIDATE"* every time you apply.

Really.

You can.

In Chapter 5 you're going to identify the work-related accomplishments of which you are most proud.

Any thoughts and feelings about being the **Meatball** or beingonelittlestrandofforgettablefettuccini?

*Learning Journal.*

## ~~ Time passes ~~

And when you've written what needs to be written, we'll get into your most meaningful accomplishments.

## CHAPTER 5

# What are your top five work accomplishments of which you are most proud?

OK. Let's recap. Here's what we've done so far:

1. A *baseline exercise*

2. Told and dispensed with your *"victim story"* and began creating a new and empowering *"story"*

3. Learned about a *"Felt Shift"*

4. Spent time in your *Learning Journal* capturing your thoughts and feelings on your *Inner Game*

5. Thought about the differences between *"Victim"* and *"Response-Able"*

6. Done a lot with *"Self-Talk"* and *"limiting beliefs"*

7. Begun to deal with the crippling limiting beliefs that *"There's no work"* and *"Nobody's hiring"*

8. Considered the differences between *"Custom"* Meatballs and *"Generic"* spaghetti

9. Started to *Update your Attitude.*

With that as the foundation, now you're going to really begin to **Win Your *Inner Game.***

## "Accomplishments" are funny things

We all have them, but we don't always acknowledge them to others, and most importantly to ourselves.

And sometimes we think so little of ourselves that we don't believe we have any at all.

And worse, even if we happen to be aware of some of them, often we don't know how to present them in our résumés and cover letters or effectively talk about them during interviews.

Or maybe we don't ever get that far because our *"Self-Talk"* squashes us like a bug, telling us something insidious like, *"Yeah, I accomplished that and I'm proud of it, but the person who could hire me will think it's trivial. So there's no point in putting it in my résumé or even applying there."*

Our negative *"Self-Talk"* is so much a part of us that we remove ourselves from consideration long before possible employers ever have a chance to.

And of course we are responsible for our prolonged unemployment.

That's tragic and sooo unnecessary.

As hockey legend Wayne Gretzky is credited with saying, (or maybe it was Michael Jordan) *"You miss 100% of the shots you don't take."*

Over the summer I worked with a former neighbor to help her move from **Generic 90%er** to **Motivated 10%er** and get back into the job market. (*Note:* She called me a couple of weeks ago to tell me she just got a job that was important to her and she wanted to thank me for our conversations. ☺)

We sat on the deck one day talking about accomplishments and after cutting through her nervous chatter as our relationship changed from neighbor and friends to résumé strategist and job coach, I asked her to open her notebook and give short titles to the top 10 accomplishments of which she was most proud, the ones that would be relevant to work she wants to do.

Her reaction to **"top 10 accomplishments"** was such that you'd have thought I asked her to wrap herself in plastic wrap and run naked around the block while dogs chased her and the neighbors shot bottle rockets at her on the Fourth of July.

In situations like this, I'm a focused and caring hammer, and uncomfortable or not, I cut no slack.

For her own self-esteem, I wanted her to identify her top 10 relevant accomplishments of which she was most proud.

Firmly on the spot and clearly uncomfortable, although it got easier as she went along, she finally made her list.

Having proven to herself that she could do ten, I asked her to take it to 20.

She did, with much less drama and increasing self-confidence, self-awareness and enthusiasm. The more we talked, the more relevant accomplishments of which she was proud bubbled up and out of her.

By the time we were done, she had identified **52** relevant accomplishments of which she was most proud.

That's *Fifty-Two!* And this from the woman who at first thought TEN would make her head explode.

As we went through the process, I was absolutely astounded to see her physical demeanor and appearance change.

Her speech became charged with positive emotion. Her eyes and facial expressions were a joy to watch as she transformed herself from tense and doubtful to energized, relaxed, spontaneous, happy, and confident.

Literally for a time her enthusiasm caused her to morph into someone else.

She was talking with me at one level while her subconscious churned away identifying other accomplishments. It was a magical sight for me to see.

She happily and repeatedly interrupted herself and me to write down the title of yet another and another accomplishment. Her conversation evolved from nervous and uncomfortable at the outset to strong and confirming as we went along.

When she started her list, I had her write *"Tastefully Boast"* at the top of the page because she felt uncomfortable bragging about herself.

Your turn. Find the first page in your *Learning Journal* where you'll do this next exercise and write *"Tastefully Boast"* at the top of the page.

As you think about and begin writing the titles of your accomplishments, do so from the perspective of *"TASTEFULLY BOASTING"* about them and about yourself.

Perhaps this will be a totally new experience for you and you may feel uncomfortable.

If so, it's time to get out of your own way, get over yourself, and get used to it.

## "That's an accomplishment. You should write that down"

In conversations with people I meet, my antenna is tuned to hear accomplishments. When I do, I may remark to the person, *"That's an accomplishment. You should write that down."*

Those who are **Motivated 10%ers** get a speculative look of curious interest in their eyes and I can see them make note of the point that prompted my observation.

Those who are **Generic 90%ers** react more slowly, scrunching up their eyes in thought, and other times my comment is entirely lost to them.

I groove on people's accomplishments and the skills they used to achieve them.

I remind you that my 35+ year career has been in domestic and international Human Resources, and for 18 of those years my responsibilities included in-house recruiting.

The résumés that caught my interest and won interviews were the ones where applicants told me about problems they had faced and fixed – in other words, their accomplishments.

The résumés that ended up in my **TBNT (Thanks But No Thanks) file** were the reverse-chronological **Job Search Junk Mail** ones - generic, boring *"dates-and-duties"* crap. Useless and unfortunate because they were a waste of both the sender's hope and energy and my time. (But at least I wasn't rude and never left them hanging. Each got a polite TBNT letter. And sometimes if I felt it might help I'd offer résumé feedback.)

## "Hello! I'm Don. I'm a recruiter"

Serendipity.

So here we are, you and I. We've just met at a party. I tell you I'm an in-house recruiter for Company X and you tell me you've just *"updated your résumé"* and applied for a job at, of all places, Company X.

Since the best recruiters are always on the look-out for bright candidates (and I was definitely one of the best,) first I'll ask what you do and what field you're in, just to give you something comfortable to start talking about.

But what I really want to get to is this: *"What's your most proud work-related accomplishment, the one that most advanced your career?"*

A short but relevant detour. Shortly after starting my first job - property HR director with Marriott Hotels - I learned to insert *"work-related"* before *"accomplishment"* because so many people looking for work replied with things like, *"the day I got married"* or *"the birth of my first child."*

That's sweet, but since you only get one chance to make an impressive, relevant and positive first impression, accomplishments like those suggested I was speaking with a clueless person with poor judgment and lack of awareness. I'm sure answers like that were intended to convey they were nice people, but *"nice person"* was never a hiring criterion of my open requisitions.

So I ask you, *"What's your most proud work-related accomplishment?"*

If you are a **Motivated 10%er,** that question is a gift. If you are a **Generic 90%er,** you'll likely blow a fine opportunity if you stare at the ceiling or your shoes and mumble something unimpressive like, *"Ummm. Good question."* Or something generic like, *"I'm really good with people."*

Give it some thought because in a few minutes you'll have an opportunity to answer that question in a critical three-part exercise.

So back to the party. We chat and at the end of our conversation, we exchange cards. If your responses were engaging, finding and reading your résumé will be a priority. If your responses were **generically "muh,"** well, I'll definitely have better things to do.

TBNT.

And BTW, particularly if you're out of work, I hope you have business cards containing at least the basics: name, address, phone and email. Because so many out-of-work people don't go to the trouble of doing that, if you do you'll make a positive impression and help recruiters remember you.

## Here's the exercise

**Assume you are prepping for an interview with me and you know I focus on accomplishments. Prep this question:** *"What's your most proud work-related accomplishment?"*

**Part 1:**

**First,** you'll give your accomplishment a short title.

**Then** you'll write a 250-word **accomplishment essay** answering these four questions:

**What** I did? **How** I did it? **Why** I did it? **Quantified results** of what I did?

This will NOT be a rehash of your *"victim"* story. (Trash-and-Recycle came today. They put on their Haz-Mat suits and hauled your toxic *"victim story"* away to the dump.)

Rather, this will be your opportunity to *"tastefully boast"* by telling a strong **Inner Game** *"story"* about a relevant accomplishment of which you are proud and that will interest me and the hiring manager in my company.

When you get into it, please take your time and do a complete job. **Your target: 250 words.**

Not 90 words. Not 187 words. Not 450 words. **Your target is 250 words.**

**Part 2:**

**Then,** you'll **analyze your essay** to make sure you answered all four questions: **What** I did? **How** I did it? **Why** I did it? **Quantified results** of what I did?

**Part 3:**

**Then** you'll synthesize your essay into a six- to eight-sentence **accomplishment statement** of between **120 – 180 words**. Generally speaking, less is more.

**Then** you'll sit back with a contented *"HOT-DAMN!-I-DID-THAT"* sigh.

Before I send you off to think, feel, remember and write *(tastefully boast)*, perhaps **an example of an effective accomplishment essay** would be helpful.

## Title: "JV Failed Because Wheeler-Dealer VP Ignored Potential People Problems"

*New to the company, I had HR responsibility for sites in New Zealand and a new joint venture in California. The VP who did the JV did a financial due diligence that ignored the people aspect. My first assignment was to "take care of the people side" of his deal. Before leaving for California, he told me about the people and positively bubbled about the new Managing Director he transferred from New Zealand. ~~~ On first visits, I have no agenda. I just walk, talk, observe and get to know folks. ~~~ People were secretive about their MD, so I probed. In just five days I identified 10 critical red flags the VP's due diligence never considered. They should have caused him to either look more closely or back away. Sharing them with him, he angrily blew me off, telling me I was new and didn't know what I was doing. ~~~ Fast forward six months. He finally saw my red flags and became concerned. Long story short, we had cause to terminate. Over my objection, he paid the MD a fat severance because it was "the* right thing to do." *I went to California and fired him on a Friday. He cashed the check faster than a hot slap and on Monday surfaced across town, now openly our competitor's Managing Director. RESULTS: my employer lost several million dollars, the JV failed, we exited the New Zealand business and the VP was fired. Lesson: Don't invest venture capital until you've analyzed human capital.* (**Word Count: 253**) – **Word counts are just for your information.**

That was my accomplishment. It happened almost 20 years ago and was important for my career. When I think of *what I did, how, why and the results*, I remember and relive the details with crystal clarity and I get all tingly proud of my accomplishment.

When you write your accomplishments essays and accomplishment statements, that's the feeling I want you to have. *Tingly proud.*

When I was in job-search mode for an HR position, I could talk authentically and effectively (*"tastefully boast"*) about *what*, *how*, *why* and the *results* for all my accomplishments.

In Chapter 6 you'll do **Parts 2 and 3.** I'll show you how to synthesize your **Accomplishment Essay** into the **Accomplishment Statement** you'll customize for use in your targeted résumés. And if you want to, you can take it even further and turn it into an **Accomplishment Bullet Point,** if that's how you want to present yourself.

For now it's your turn to **write your first Accomplishment Essay**. Gather your thoughts, let yourself remember and feel again how wonderful that success felt.

If what you're going to write about happened as part of a team, focus on YOUR ROLE and YOUR ACHIEVEMENT or YOUR CONTRIBUTION to the end result. It's good that you were a team player, but right now the hiring manager wants to know what YOU did, not what the team did.

Relive it. Don't be shy. Don't be modest,. Don't hold back. **Do** *"Tastefully Boast."*

Roll all this around in your head and then get to it.

**Part 1:**

## Your first Accomplishment Essay

Remember:

Around **250 words: WHAT** you did / **HOW** you did it / **WHY** you did it / **QUANTIFIED RESULTS**

## ~~ Time Passes ~~

Welcome back!

How was that? Did you love what you wrote? Could you feel it in your bones? Did you find yourself feeling all warm and glowy inside? Did you start to *"see"* yourself a little differently?

If so, EXCELLENT! Before we're done, I'm going to ask you to identify and write up a minimum of five accomplishments of which you are proud. Ten would be better and 20 would confirm to yourself that you are indeed a *Motivated 10%er* over-achiever and would send me over-the-moon.

*However,* if you did not feel all *tingly proud*, I'd like you to try again.

Use your positive *"Self-Talk."* **Don't quit on yourself.** This is your life we're talking about.

Make it work.

## If your "Self-Talk" is screaming "NO BIG DEAL", try this

Grab an old pair of thick socks and roll them into a ball. Cover it in duck tape and in large block letters print the words *NEGATIVE "SELF-TALK."* Slap it around the house. Kick it around the back yard. Stomp on it and abuse it. Let the dog pee on it. When you've had enough, throw it into the garbage, preferably into something really slimy and yucky. Whip out your cell phone and take a close-up photo of it lying in its bed of sucky yuck. Before you take the picture, make sure you can read the words and if they're smeared with gunk, that's great! After you have a good photo, post it where you can see it. Toss some more garbage on the sock ball just for good measure and leave it for the trash pick-up. When you find yourself and your *"Self-Talk"* going down the tubes, reconnect with the photo and relive this moment.

## Either redo your first accomplishment essay or write a different one

Remember: *"How you do anything is how you do everything,"* so for this essay and the others you'll do later, load them with emotion, *"uumpf,"* passion and what I call *"thought muscle."*

Don't just go through the motions by superficially thinking and writing about something generic, trivial or boring. You'll get lethargic and end up yawning your way into a nap to escape your boredom. If *you're* bored with you, the recruiter or hiring manager will be absolutely catatonic.

That will defeat the whole purpose of this *Workbook*. Your ***Inner Game*** will remain flaccid, anemic, floating face-down dead in the water. In a word, ***"muh."***

Before you go on to Chapter 6, I want to give you every opportunity to make sure you've experienced real enthusiasm for an accomplishment and gotten yourself out of what I think of as **The Dead Zone.**

## ~~~Time Passes~~~

If your first essay was *"all-that-and-a-bag-of-chips,"* let's close out this chapter.

Enough *"tasteful boasting"* for the moment.

If things have gone as I hope, you'll be feeling pretty *"chipper"* (Get it? *"Bag of Chips?"* *"Chipper?"* Hahaha. Ahem.) just about now, maybe sitting there with a big dopey grin going, *"YEAH! I'm all-that-AND-a-bag-of-chips! That accomplishment is ME! It's MINE! I'm THAT!"*

I do apologize for that bad joke, but not all that much because it made me giggle.

## By now you've written one, or maybe two, essays

I'm assuming you're now excited and all tingly-pleased with yourself, so while your ***Inner Game*** is in overdrive and your thoughts and feelings are fresh, please go to your *Learning Journal* and answer these initial questions that will contribute to the initial framework of **your Plan** that we will get to in Chapter 8.

1. How are you feeling about the essay(s) you just wrote? Why?

2. When was the last time you felt like this?

3. Do you want to keep feeling like this? Why?

4. What do you need to do right now to keep feeling this feeling? Next week? Next month?

5. Note the basic elements of **your Plan** to continue to feel like this. (Details will come later)

6. Before you put this aside and take a 24-hour break, what is the ONE WORD that describes how you are feeling right this second? Why?

## ~~~Time Passes~~~

## GOOD JOB, YOU!

Now please close the book and go do something else.

Before you go . . . While on your break, just sort of think about your remaining top nine (did you see how I slipped that new target number in there? Smooth, huh? *"Nine"* because what I'd really like you to write are 10 (at least) relevant accomplishment essays and statements of which you are most proud.)

We are going to tackle them next.

While on your break, you might want to jot them down so you'll remember them tomorrow.

Later, Tater.

## But Wait! There's more

If you're still not all that happy, excited and impressed with yourself, you have some thinking work to do over the next 24 hours.

You need to change your state of mind and your emotional state because I don't want you writing accomplishment essays *while you are playing a losing Inner Game.*

Go do something fun and legal that gets you positively stoked.

Then come back and redo Chapter 5.

Don't just *"settle,"* because that's about the same as *quitting on yourself.*

**And do not proceed to Chapter 6 until** you have written at least one accomplishment essay in which you have truly *"tastefully boasted"* and *you can feel the pride and joy of accomplishment bouncing around inside you.*

# CHAPTER 6

# Turning Your *Accomplishment Essay* into an Accomplishment *Statement*

OK! I hope you did as I asked and pretty much *"chillaxed"* or reworked Chapter 5 to the point that you *"tastefully boasted"* and were sincerely impressed with yourself, and then *"chillaxed."*

You did do one or the other – yes?

Good.

Nice word, *"chillaxed."*

Break time is now officially over and I'm committed to maintaining your positive momentum to the end.

My D-I-Y system of helping you to stand out like a MEATBALL on a pile of generic spaghetti is based on identifying your most relevant professional accomplishments and the skills you used to achieve them.

Since your **Inner Game** is based primarily on your accomplishments, that's our focus.

After you have completed the *Workbook,* you'll be ready for ***How to Get Interviews! Stop Sending Job Search Junk Mail.*** There you'll learn more about your **Representative Professional Accomplishments**, your **Special Skills and Abilities** and how to create custom **Objective Statements** so you can present yourself as an **"Ideal Candidate"** each time you apply.

Did I mention that **Stop Sending Junk Search Junk Mail** was an Amazon Kindle Best Seller? That's an accomplishment I'm pretty proud of.

Back to you.

One of the primary benefits of writing a comprehensive **Accomplishment Essay** that answers all four questions is that it prepares you to interview effectively. Therefore, I want to make sure you've answered all four questions.

## Analyzing your Accomplishment Essay

**Part 2.**

This is the intermediate step between writing your **Accomplishment Essay** and then writing your **Accomplishment Statement.**

It's also a fine opportunity to reinforce and recognize the thoroughness and commitment of a *Motivated 10%er.*

Why? Because many times a **Generic 90%er** will think this step is superfluous and skip it, blithely and unthinkingly thinking they've written a complete essay. Then when we review it together they realize what they wrote is incomplete (mediocre) because they left out critical data, were superficial in their thinking and pretty much wasted their time.

**How you do anything is how you do everything.**

I'll demonstrate the analysis using my earlier **Accomplishment Statement.**

Here are the four questions I wanted to answer in my **Accomplishment Essay**. If you are using a Kindle, please match content with color. For those of you reading this in a book or using a black-and-white reader, I put the questions in parenthesis.

# WHAT I did   HOW I did it   WHY I did it
# QUANTIFIED RESULTS

*New to the company, I had HR responsibility for sites in New Zealand and a new joint venture in California. The VP who did the JV did a financial due diligence that ignored the people aspect. (What) My first assignment was to "take care of the people side" of his deal. Before leaving for California, he told me about the people and positively bubbled about the new managing director he transferred from New Zealand. ~~~ (How) On first visits, I have no agenda. I just walk, talk, observe and get to know folks. ~~~ (Why) People were secretive about their MD, so I probed. (Results) In just five days I identified 10 critical red flags the VP's due diligence never considered. They should have made him either look more closely or back away. Sharing them with him, he angrily blew me off, telling me I was new and didn't know what I was doing. ~~~ Fast forward six months. He saw my red flags and became concerned. Long story short, (What) we had cause to terminate. Over my objection, he paid the MD a fat severance because it was "the right thing to do." (What) I went to California and fired him on a Friday. He cashed the check faster than a hot slap and the following Monday (Results) surfaced across town, now openly our competitor's managing director. RESULTS:*

*my employer lost several million dollars, the JV failed, we exited the New Zealand business and the VP was fired. Lesson: Don't invest venture capital until you've analyzed human capital.*

# Writing your Accomplishment Statement

**Part 3.**

And from my earlier Accomplishment Essay, here's my **Accomplishment Statement** that I'd store in my **Accomplishments Data Bank**:

*Ignoring the people side of a joint venture can get you fired. As the new Asia-Pacific HR manager, my first assignment was to manage the people part of a new JV between our New Zealand company and a new California partner. Before my first California trip, the VP deal-maker told me I was going to love the Managing Director he relocated from our New Zealand company. Employees opened up to me about everything except the new MD. Probing, I uncovered 10 critical people red flags the VP's financial due diligence never considered. Abusively angry at me when I shared my findings, it took him six months to see what I saw in five days. I fired the MD on a Friday. Over my objection the VP made me give him a $50K severance check, which he immediately cashed. The following Monday he surfaced as our competition's MD. By ignoring the people side of the deal, we lost several million dollars, the JV failed, we exited New Zealand, and the VP was fired. Undetected people issues kill deals and careers.* **(Word Count: 179)**

**To see a second essay analyzed using the** *"Comments"* **feature in WORD, go to stopsendingjobsearchjunkmail.com/analyze-accomplishment-essay/**

As you saw, you don't need to use the exact words from the **Accomplishment Essay** in your **Accomplishment Statement**. What you do want to do is make sure you have answered all four questions in an authentic style that is *"you."*

There is no set format to write the **Accomplishment Statement.** Before I start I decide on the main point I want to make and lead with that – in this case, *"Ignoring the people side of a JV can get you fired."*

And from there I just tell the story in as few words as possible, providing enough detail to keep it interesting and trying to stay under or near 180 words.

If you decide you don't want to use an **Accomplishment Statement** (which I prefer because it gives more flexibility to customize) you could refine it into an **Accomplishment Bullet Point.**

For example:

> *Angering the VP deal-maker, in my first assignment I identified 10 "people" red flags in a recent multi-national joint venture that his financial due diligence never considered. Within a year those red flags killed the deal. My employer lost several million dollars, severed relations with the other two companies and the VP deal-maker was fired. An unfortunate but effective way to gain professional credibility.* **(Word Count: 64)**

The Word Counts are not for inclusion. They are just there for your information.

As you add **Accomplishment Statements** to your **Accomplishment Data Bank**, it's important to organize it by subcategories.

Possible subcategories for this **Accomplishment Statement** could be:

1.  *HR's Role in Mergers, Acquisitions and Joint Ventures*

2.  *Financial AND People: A Complete Due Diligence*

3.  *Analyze Human Capital Before Investing Financial Capital, or*

4.  *Potential People Problems Can Kill Joint Ventures*

You get the idea – yes?

## GOOD!

In Chapter 7, you and your relevant professional accomplishments will take center stage.

# CHAPTER 7

# Your Accomplishment Essays and Accomplishment Statements

In this Chapter, you and your *Learning Journal* will spend a lot of time together.

Before you get into some serious thinking and writing, I want to give you **five successful accomplishment statements** that worked for their users.

1. This first one is a favorite of mine. It helped a young woman establish a degree of *"remote control"* with her interviewers and make her memorable to them, even before she met them. Notice the **bold text** at the end.

## COST-CONSCIOUS, HANDS-ON CREATIVITY

*After planning everything to the $n^{th}$ degree, I experienced the **BEST THREE DAYS OF MY LIFE** – my wedding. From the tiara to the train of my dress to the table arrangements – I planned everything, and had hands-on involvement in most of it as well. Everything within my control went just as I had envisioned it. Why is my wedding an accomplishment for my résumé? Because by utilizing my contacts with the industry and the area, and by doing many things myself, I created an elegant $15,500 wedding for only $8,371, a savings of $6,629. **I promise you that I am just as detail-oriented and cost-conscious when it comes to spending my employer's money as I am with my own.** (WC: 119)*

2. I'm very proud of this next one. A student graduated with a BS in Physics and Laser Optics. Following the guidance from his Career Services office and with final approval of his counsellor, he prepared and sent out a couple hundred generic reverse-chronological résumés. Career Services told him that company recruiters wanted résumés in that format because it made it easier for them to review. Unintentionally his Career Services office turned him into spaghetti. He went for over three months without an interview. Not one.

Compounding that, when we first started working together, the only accomplishment he could identify was that he graduated. Not one single adult on campus suggested he think about and position his labs, projects, dorm, and campus activities in terms of accomplishments of possible interest to employers. That is a travesty for which people who called themselves *"professionals"* collected paychecks. After he got learned my system and began presenting his accomplishments in an interesting and relevant manner, he began getting interviews.

## RESEARCH, DEVELOP, BUILD AND TEST LASERS

*Labview Driver: As part of my Senior Project (Spatial-Spectral Hole Recovery), as a check on the accuracy of the simulated results I obtained, I simulated white light and random noise inside an S2 crystal by changing a voltage across the crystal that can be easily controlled. After finding a complete Labview driver online, and then adding the ability to read text files of voltage outputs, I had it use the outputs to create an arbitrary wave and remove the not-required additions. Since this was the first time I had created a Labview driver on my own, I had to teach myself the programming and supporting subroutines. I was able to confirm that the data was being simulated correctly. (WC: 118)*

3.    This man is a Baby Boomer. His company merged and after training his replacement, his position went away and so did he. After he was laid off he used a traditional generic reverse-chronological résumé and went for months without an interview. After working my system and customizing his credentials to the requirements of one specific position, he was an *"Ideal Candidate"* for an Organization Development management position. He submitted his packet and was immediately contacted. After going through the phone screen and all-day on-site interviews, he came in second.

No problem, because he immediately and easily **selected and repurposed** different accomplishment statements and skills from his Data Banks and presented himself as an *"Ideal Candidate"* to teach Organization Development at his local university. He was interviewed at once and was hired.

Hiring managers for both positions complimented him on the thoroughness of his six- – that's s-i-x – page résumé.

So much for that two-page maximum BS.

**Be the Meatball, not the spaghetti.**

## PROFITABILITY THROUGH TRAINING DESIGN AND DELIVERY

*At the Richmond plant, I introduced a 10-step OD change management model that became the foundation for benchmarking practices of our High-Performing Work System (HPWS). Lack of a common language hampered our ability to meet our two primary goals: shipping product and being in compliance with Home Office and FDA/OSHA mandates. Under the umbrella of creating a unified plant-wide work system, I facilitated each of the 35 work teams (26 managers and >350 employees) to create their own complimentary processes to implement HPWS. My team facilitation and internal consulting resulted in more effective working relationships among Operations, Procurement and Quality Assurance/Control such that we met all of our Home Office obligations while being in full compliance with all government mandates. (WC: 120)*

4.  This multimedia filmmaker is a multitalented entrepreneurial man of unlimited creativity. After 15 years of working for others he decided it was time to go out on his own. Using my strategy of asking his network for referrals (not a job – referrals) he put together a résumé highlighting the accomplishments of which he was most proud and sent it to his network. They responded with referrals and he found himself with several contracting opportunities.

## REVENUE GENERATION

*During my year with Company, I generated the most revenue ($130,000) of any producer in Washington State. I accomplished this by always thinking ahead as I balanced multiple projects and internal and external vendors at any given time. I utilized my time with each client very judiciously, was hyper-aware of making budget, and continually checked with clients and my management to make sure nothing fell between the cracks. During that year, I produced well over two hundred commercials and two large Video-On-Demand projects. (WC: 83)*

5.  By age 21, this young man was a published author and an accomplished motivational speaker with the mission of helping kids either get out or stay out of gangs. His story is critical to this *Workbook*.

We met while he was writing his first book. He was also going to school and working in retail sales to support himself and help his mother and cousin.

A quick learner, he was caught in a Catch-22 because the only résumés he knew were generic reverse-chronological ones, and hiring managers and recruiters routinely ignored the ones he sent in. He quickly learned my D-I-Y system and now can get interviews whenever he wants them.

A believer in paying-it-forward, he shared a draft of an earlier book with ten of his friends, all of whom were in the same Catch-22. All had been using generic reverse-chronological résumés and recruiters ignored them all. All ten read the draft. Eight said it was *"too difficult"* and went back to sending out the same résumés recruiters routinely ignored. The ninth created a targeted résumé and cover letter but did not send it because it made him look *"too different."*

Imagine the turmoil of their ***"Inner Games."*** Those nine were **Generic 90%ers** who **quit on themselves.**

The tenth was a ***Motivated 10%er.*** He liked his new look on paper, liked how he felt about himself, submitted his targeted credentials and within a week was interviewed, hired and started work.

**Meatball,** notforgettablefettuccini.

This was one of my friend's earliest accomplishment statements.

## A COMMITMENT TO DOING IT RIGHT

*While working at the respiratory care company, on some occasions customers would call and tell me that sleeping was even more difficult because their mask was bothering them. One customer in particular stands out. He had been adamant in his selection of an oxygen mask that went into the nostrils and now he complained that it hurt him. Without dwelling on his insistence on that model, I suggested that a full-face mask that covered the nose and mouth would probably be better.*

*We went online to our website and I showed him the full-face masks we had available and he selected his new mask. I sent it to him and followed up shortly thereafter. He was delighted with the mask and with the good sleep he had gotten. By helping him find the right mask and not making him feel like he had made a mistake the first time, he signed on for a higher-priced maintenance program we offered, and referred others to us as well. (WC: 166)*

OK. I could give you example after example until your eyes crossed, and I think you get the idea.

## Analyze your first essay and write the Accomplishment Statement

Please **analyze your first essay** and then write your corresponding **Accomplishment Statement.** Do the bullet point version if you wish.

## ~~ Time Passes ~~

By the time you're done with this chapter, I'd like you to please have a minimum of **five complete packets.** That will get you accustomed to the process and you'll be prepared to take it to the next level in *How to Get Interviews! Stop Sending Job Search Junk Mail.* The more packets you have, the better off you'll be.

**Each packet will contain:**

1. An **Accomplishment Essay**

2. An **Analysis** of your Accomplishment Essay

3. A completed **Accomplishment Statement** or **bullet point** for your Accomplishment Data Bank

## Instructions:

Before you get started writing your remaining four, write the short titles of each **Accomplishment Essay** in your *Learning Journal* and then **your first packet.**

## ~~ Time passes ~~

When you've finished that **first packet,** save it and leave the *Workbook.* Take a break for a bit but think about what you wrote. When you come back, review the first packet and make any adjustments you feel are needed.

Then write the **remaining four Accomplishment Essays**.

**After you've finished all the Essays,** go back and do the four **analyses** and **Accomplishment Statements.**

## Your turn.

Please head for your *Learning Journal*. Your goal is five complete packets, each consisting of an effectively-written **Accomplishment Essay**, an **Analysis of your essay** to be certain you have answered the four questions, and your **Accomplishment statement** that you'll keep in your **Accomplishments Data Bank.**

See you when you're done.

## ~~ Time Passes ~~

## WELCOME BACK!

## Wow! Lot of work – yes?

Quick dip into your *Learning Journal.*

1.  How are you feeling? Tired? Invigorated? Impressed with yourself? All of that and some more too?

2.  What else?

## ~~ Time Passes ~~

Up next - the final chapter.

And before you get there – let's make sure you've taken care of some little leftovers.

Have you created and saved your **Accomplishments Data Bank** as a Word document? If not, please do so now, before you move on.

And remember to organize your **Accomplishment Statements** into logical subcategories. As your **Accomplishment Data Bank** grows with your career, you'll be glad you organized it effectively right from the start.

## ~~ Time passes ~~

In Chapter 8 we'll bring it all together.

Some people charge right through this and the process energizes them; and for others, it is draining.

If your energy is low at this moment, I recommend you do something else to recharge your battery and come back to finish it off when you're rested and fresh.

You're getting so very close – I'd like you fresh and alert for the final chapter because it is all going to come together with a bang!

## CHAPTER 8

# / Ideal / Actual / Obstacles / Plan /

Well, here we are.

Think a minute about all you've accomplished to get here.

And now the end is in sight.

At the end of the last chapter I asked how you were feeling after all that work.

Now I'm asking you . . .

## How you are feeling about "YOU"?

In your *Learning Journal*, please answer these questions:

1.  Think back to how you were feeling when you started the *Workbook* - on a scale of 0 to 10 (low to high) how impressed with yourself were you then?

2.  And how impressed are you with "YOU" right now?

3.  On a scale of 0 to 10 right now, for each of these six elements, where's your:

a. Your Spirit?
b. Your energy?
c. Your self-confidence?
d. Your self-esteem?
e. Your optimism about getting interviews for meaningful work you want to do?
**f. Your overall *Inner Game***

4.  If you did not give yourself all *"10's,"* why? What still needs to be done to get it there?

5.  How will you make that happen? Whose help will you need? How will you get it?

## ~~ Time passes ~~

We're coming down the home stretch, and if you haven't quit on yourself by just slapping down any old bunch of words so you could say you did it or to get somebody off your back, by now I hope you're starting to see yourself through different eyes, and are liking what you see.

If you are, then you must be feeling pretty proud of yourself – the way *Motivated 10%ers* feel when they keep their word to themselves and others and do the meaningful thing they said they'd do.

I hope you're starting to see and feel the power of getting clear on your *relevant professional accomplishments* and how much more likely you are to win interviews when you use them to present yourself as a *"Meatball Ideal Candidate"* rather than continue going *"dates-and-duties"* and blendinginasjustanotherpieceof*GenericSpaghettiJobSearchJunkMail*.

I love the concept of being the MEATBALL and not the spaghetti.

Why? Because **MEATBALLS** get calls and spaghetti gets forked.

Repeat after me: "CUSTOM" Works. "GENERIC" Remains Unemployed.

*Generic 90%ers* remain on the outside looking in at the *Motivated 10%ers* who get interviews and some get hired.

And for that reason I hope you're now taking long strides out of the *Generic 90%er* camp and joining the *Motivated 10%ers.*

As we go into the last Chapter, I remind you to please keep this concept in mind.

This is how hiring managers see your boring, generic, mass-distributed resume.

"Generic"
remains unemployed

"Custom"
works

This is how hiring managers see your professional profile customized to the specific requirements of their job

*Be the **Meatball**. Don't blendinliketheforgetablefettuccini.*

*Generic 90%ers* get lost in the bowl. *Motivated 10%ers* STAND OUT.

All right. Let's lay out **your** / *Ideal* / *Actual* / *Obstacles* / *Plan* / **PLAN FOR YOUR FUTURE.**

You've done a lot of honest self-examination over the last seven chapters. If you've trusted the process and worked it to the best of your ability (and not just skipped to the end) I'm going to believe you've experienced a positive shift (maybe even a *"Felt Shift"*) in how you see yourself.

Your self-confidence and self-esteem have increased. You've **Updated your Attitude.** You have a new sense of optimism about **Your** *Inner Game* and **your prospects for playing a stronger Outer Game.**

And along the way, you may have even chosen to become a ***Motivated 10%er.***

We're now going to capitalize on that positive momentum by developing a practical, realistic plan to help you win your ***Inner Game,*** be an IDEAL CANDIDATE and get interviews.

I'm going to share a four-step process I have used successfully over 100 times in the last 35+ years to help individuals and teams sort out conflicts, issues and problems so they can successfully transition across the gap from *where they are* to *where they want to be.*

I learned this process from a great man - my boss, James "Bud" Ward, civil rights pioneer and Corporate Vice President of Organization Development at Marriott Hotels. He called an ***"Ideal Profile Process"*** and this is the first time I've presented it like this, without actually facilitating it, so we are both pioneers and together we're taking something of a risk.

I'm going to give you an example of how the process works and then invite you to do it yourself.

## The "Ideal Profile"

What follows is an example of a completed ***IDEAL PROFILE***. If we were doing this together, I'd be using a flip-chart to take us through the four steps:

1. **IDEAL**
2. **ACTUAL**
3. **OBSTACLES**
4. **PLAN**

**Overview of the Process:** If we were doing this real-time, I would prepare the charts like this:

| IDEAL | ACTUAL                                    P. 1 |
|-------|-----------------------------------------------|
|       |                                               |
|       |                                               |
|       |                                               |

Divided in half vertically and numbered consecutively, the left half of a number of pages would be titled **IDEAL.** The right half of the pages – **ACTUAL.**

After we have defined all elements of the **IDEAL** and then done a parallel analysis to determine the **ACTUAL**, we would follow the same dual-page layout with the remaining two categories:

| OBSTACLES | PLAN                                    P. xx |
|-----------|-----------------------------------------------|
|           |                                               |
|           |                                               |
|           |                                               |

Since the intent of this process is to **help you win your** *"Inner Game"* as the first step to getting interviews, we would begin by defining the **IDEAL** and the **ACTUAL** with these questions:

| | P 1 |
|---|---|
| *IDEALLY, how to you want to feel as you conduct your search for meaningful work you want to do?* | *ACTUALLY, this is how things are with me right now* |

We will complete each category before moving to the next: **IDEAL,** then **ACTUAL,** then **OBSTACLES,** then **PLAN.**

So you could give them some thought, I would have given you the **IDEAL** and **ACTUAL** questions the day before.

In our session, I'd encourage you to speak freely and answer my questions in as much detail as possible. I'd record your answers as alphabetical bullet points on as many pages as necessary.

After we have exhausted the **IDEAL,** we would then complete a parallel analysis of each **IDEAL** alphabetical bullet point to identify how things **ACTUALLY** are vs. the **IDEAL.**

This is critical stuff, so we will take our time, being thoughtful, patient, and thorough.

As facilitator, my job is to encourage you to really open up and make sure I record what you really mean.

Under no circumstances do I want superficial, lazy or *Generic 90%er* answers.

In real time I'd complete **IDEAL** and the corresponding **ACTUAL** opposite on the same page, so that **IDEAL Item A** corresponded with **ACTUAL Item A** and all the way through to the last **Item.**

## THE EXAMPLE FOLLOWS:

# IDEAL PROFILE - / IDEAL / ACTUAL /

| IDEAL | ACTUAL |
|---|---|
| **Ideally, how to you want to feel as you conduct your search for meaningful work you want to do?** | **In Actuality, this is how things are for me right now:** |
| *A. Confident and with my self-esteem intact* | *A. When they talk on the TV news about the economy and the current unemployment level, I change channels. I psych myself out enough with the "gloom-and-doom" I create for myself – I don't need to hear it from them* |
| *B. Believing it will not take long for me to find meaningful work I want to do (in three months, before my savings are gone)* | *B. My optimism comes and goes. Sometimes I think this is just a speed-bump and other times I worry it will last forever* |
| *C. Upbeat spirit, even in the face of rejection or never hearing back from the résumés I submit* | *C. Nothing works like it used to. Before I could send the same résumé to 10 companies and be sure of at least one interview. Now I have sent 68 and not one call for an interview. Getting scared.* |
| *D. "Self-Talk" supportive and empowering* | *D. My "Self-Talk" sucks. I wish my yappy little voice had laryngitis. The tape that most often plays in my head tells me "You'll never get another job. You're going to be on welfare and food stamps and live under a bridge for the rest of your life." And like that.* |
| *E. Supported by family and friends and grateful for their referrals and invitations to dinner now-and-again* | *E. At first everyone was supportive, optimistic and encouraging. Friends and family would call to check in or invite me over. Now, I make them uncomfortable and they stay away. It's like I have a rash* |
| *F. I can put on a strong and effective "phone face" when I make calls to recruiters and hiring managers* | *F. I have to psych myself up for every call I make, and the more times I get put down, the harder that is to do. Mostly they ignore me.* |
| *G. With enough courage to try non-traditional job search methods, like writing to the CEO to ask for referrals and by-passing HR completely* | *G. When I tell people I'm thinking of being a little ballsy and sending my accomplishments résumé / cover letter to CEOs and screw HR (they never respond anyway), people tell me I'm making a mistake. I like it is different and I'm scared of making a mistake. I dither and do nothing.* |
| *H. Confident I'm not making a HUGE mistake by ignoring people who tell me my résumé "must" be no more than two pages, or that it "must" be reverse-chronology-based* | *H. I'm fearful. I keep "updating my résumé" and keep it at two pages, but it is just a rehash of the same old "dates-and-duties" crap, and I get no calls for interviews. I can do the jobs I seek.* |

| IDEAL | ACTUAL |
|---|---|
| *I. Confident in "tastefully boasting" about my accomplishments and skills. Sound believable, credible and authentic* | *I. Some people say to include accomplishments in my résumé and others say HR and recruiters distrust résumés based on accomplishments and only want to see chronological ones. I have gaps and a bunch of recent short-term jobs to carry me over, so when I lead with that, I think that's why no one calls me. I look like a job jumper. It's not me! It's the economy, Stupid!* |
| *J. Calm, confident, patient and thoughtful in how I run my job search, not all panicky and herky-jerky changing my résumé and approach each time someone hocks up a new opinion* | *J. The local State Job Source office is useless because they insist I use a reverse-chronological résumé, and all the HR departments ignore the résumés they tell me to create. My neighbor told me he included an Objective in my résumé and got an interview; my sister told me her hair dresser told her she read an article in the local paper that it is no longer needed and by omitting it HR would consider me for different jobs. I keep doing what everyone says and still no interviews.* |
| *K. That my skills and accomplishments are still relevant enough that someone will pay me for what I can do* | *K. The longer I'm out, the more obsolete, useless and unemployable I feel I am. Driving to work, I used to look with curiosity at folks sleeping under the freeway and wonder what it's like to live like that. Things keep going this way, I'll probably find out.* |

~~~

So. The first half of the *IDEAL PROFILE* process is done.

What do you think of the information contained in the **IDEAL** and **ACTUAL** columns? Does it sound like *"you"*?

**STRAIGHT TALK.** I realize some of the entries may be kind of *"crunchy"* and perhaps you have difficulty imaging yourself writing some of those things.

Get over yourself. Now.

Just get over yourself and whatever may be left of your *"story."* If you're going to move from being a **lost-in-the-crowd-spaghetti-*Generic-90%er*,** and become a *Motivated 10%er* **meatball,** you first have to be honest with yourself. Unless you choose to share what you write, no one will ever read it.

Only you. So please, be in integrity with yourself.

If we were working together, after **IDEAL/ACTUAL** we'd do lunch, and then complete **OBSTACLES/PLAN.**

While you finished your lunch and before starting the afternoon session, for clarity and ease of typing I'd edit out redundancies and hang all the **IDEAL/ACTUAL** pages high up on the wall so we can refer to them as we complete **OBSTACLES** and **PLAN**. As I completed each new **OBSTACLES/PLAN** page, I'd hang it under the corresponding **IDEAL/ACTUAL** page.

To streamline the final two steps, you'll see I've combined multiple **IDEAL/ACTUAL** to complete the **OBSTACLES** column. You don't need to do it that way. Since there were similarities, I chose to combine them.

That will carry over into / **PLAN** / as well.

## IDEAL PROFILE: / OBSTACLES / PLAN /

| OBSTACLES | PLAN |
|---|---|
| **Summary - Items A, B, C and D:** | **Specifics - Items A, B, C and D:** |
| *I spend too much time in my head, listening to my "gloom-and-doom" "Self-Talk" and continually rehashing my own miserable situation. I'm rapidly driving myself nuts because I continually focus on all the horrible things that could happen, rather than taking positive steps to extract my head from a dark place and then focus on solutions, not problems* | ***A-D 1.*** *Finish How to Get Interviews! Stop Sending Job Search Junk Mail by* <u>*DATE*</u><br><br>***A-D 2.*** *Explore YouTube for free motivational videos. Spend the first hour of each day on them and daily affirmations.*<br><br>***A-D 3.*** *Read Napoleon Hill's **Think and Grow Rich** and **Law of Success** or watch them on YouTube*<br><br>***A-D 4.*** *For "Self-Talk", start with Shad Helmstetter YouTube link to **"The Story of Self-Talk"** and book **Self-Talk Solution*** |

| OBSTACLES | PLAN |
|---|---|
| **Summary - Items E and F:**<br><br>*My "Self-Talk" again. My self-confidence and self-esteem are the pits. I'm doing it to myself. I'm embarrassed about my situation and believe I make others uncomfortable, so they avoid me. And since I feel desperate, I think I come across that way to the few recruiters I have spoken. Nobody wants to interview "desperate."* | **Specifics - Items E and F:**<br><br>*E-F 1. Decide who I know that is the most: business-savvy, compassionate, trustworthy and honest*<br><br>*E-F 2. Ask that person if they'd be willing to review this document and Workbook and give me their honest feedback and recommendations on me and what I've done*<br><br>*E-F 3. And if they are willing, ask if they would role-play some practice interviews with me, give me feedback and practice some more*<br><br>*E-F 4. Stop sending out résumés and the transparent ploy of asking for "informational interviews." Dedicate all my efforts to finishing this process and to be the "Ideal Candidate"* |
| **Summary - Items G, H, I and J:**<br><br>*Timidity about taking a risk, and listening to what "they" say. When my little voice says something courageous, I slap it down out of fear and indecisiveness. What if I'm wrong? Taking shelter again and again by following the **"Boilerplate Herd"** and they're just as screwed up as I am. I'm uncomfortable being the MEATBALL* | **Specifics - Items G, H, I and J:**<br><br>*G-J 1. Check www.**BizJournals**.com and see if they publish a **Business Journal** for my city or where I want to go. If so, use the **Book of Lists** for that city to identify employers.*<br><br>*G-J 2. Put together a résumé made up of my most proud accomplishments / skills (elements of my "Ideal Job") and a targeted cover letter asking for referrals, not a job*<br><br>*G-J 3. Get over myself and send it to a bunch of CEOs.*<br><br>*G-J 4. Really – what harm can it do? Nothing else is working*<br><br>*G-J 5. Consider using **The Directory of Executive and Professional Recruiters*** |
| **OBSTACLE Item K:**<br><br>*Talking myself into an early grave by doing all the wrong things* | **Item K:**<br><br>*K 1. Implement this PLAN – not tomorrow. Today. Now!* |

## So. / **IDEAL / ACTUAL / OBSTACLES / PLAN /**

You now have an example of a powerful, practical, authentic and effective planning process. None of what you just read is fiction.

I wanted to model the kind of real content and honest emotion I want you to create so rather than just make something up I drew on my past experiences and those that clients shared with me.

## Some guidelines to successfully complete the Ideal Profile Process

In a couple of minutes it will be your turn.

I recommend you use my initial **IDEAL** question. If you have one that fits your situation even better, use it, but do so with this caution:

When you get the initial question right, everything flows naturally, completely and effectively. And of course if you don't you'll go off on a tangent, spinning your wheels, wasting your energy and creating frustration.

Please be as thorough as possible when you complete the **IDEAL** column.

If you're thorough and honest with this process, I believe you'll find the **ACTUAL** element will be the most difficult to write because you'll be looking into the mirror of *"you."* And if you're not going to be honest with yourself, what's the point?

If you've been thorough with **ACTUAL**, I think you'll find the **OBSTACLES** element maybe a little less challenging. Once you've completed it equally thoroughly and honestly, you can expect that big weight you've been carrying around for a long time to lift off your shoulders.

And the **PLAN** column is almost fun because it's like opening a door from a dark cell and stepping out into freedom.

I say *"almost"* because you're making a promise to yourself, a commitment, and one of the traits of a *Motivated 10%er* is that they keep their commitments.

Give a lot of thought to what you're willing to do because *I don't want you to quit on yourself.*

More importantly, it's imperative that by now, **you** *don't want to quit on yourself*, either.

What I'm suggesting is that you give yourself some creative thinking time. Make the **PLAN** column of your **IDEAL PROFILE** a stretch without trying to eat the elephant in one bite. As you get comfortable with the process and successfully achieve the **PLAN** goals of your first **Ideal Profile**, do another complete **Ideal Profile Process** and make the **PLAN** column incrementally more challenging.

Completed and implemented with intention and commitment, what you write in these four columns may well be **the blueprint to getting your life back on-track.**

**Instructions to complete your *IDEAL PROFILE* (Ideal/Actual/Obstacles/Plan)**

**FIRST: Before you begin** *your IDEAL PROFILE,* let's lay the foundation for your success by giving your brain and your heart something tangible to work with.

*Learning Journal.*

1.  *Please review your answers to all of the questions* in this *Workbook,* including your original *"Story."* Doing so will give you food for thought and you'll realize just so how far you've come.

Keep your notes handy so you can use them to complete your **IDEAL PROFILE.**

**SECOND:** Please set aside at least four to five hours of undisturbed time to start and complete your *Ideal Profile process* in one sitting. No outside interruption – no phones, no pets, no family.

Just you.

Maybe make it a special event and go to a place that's special to you.

When I want to do something important like this, I take a thermos of coffee and go to a picnic table at my favorite campsite. This is my view, and I'm just out of cellphone range:

Photo by Don Burrows

Make it meaningful and important.

Like any effective plan, your **Ideal Profile Process** needs to be fact- and reality-based.

The **IDEAL, ACTUAL** and **OBSTACLES** are fact- and reality-based. And the **PLAN** column should meet the *S.M.A.R.T.* criteria of *Specific. Measurable. Actionable. Relevant. Timely.* It is also where you get creative and a little daring.

**STRAIGHT TALK.** I've provided you with a complete *Ideal Profile* to show you how the process works. I know you won't but I felt the need to say that under no circumstances should you to take what I've written and simply copy it. That's maybe *'old you' Generic 90%er behavior* – now longggg behind you.

Instead, it's time for your own original *Inner Game* thinking.

At least for your first time, I encourage you to use this *Inner Game IDEAL* question, because as you can see, it works:

*"IDEALLY, how to you want to feel as you conduct your search for meaningful work you want to do?"*

Don't go superficial or mediocre and above all, don't go *"Victim."*

Do the work. Stretch and dream as you define all the pieces of your own **IDEAL.**

Level with yourself. Feel, face and embrace the pain of your own **ACTUAL.**

Identify and acknowledge the truth of your own **OBSTACLES**, *particularly those you knowingly or unknowingly created for yourself.*

Use the first three elements to think and feel broadly, deeply and honestly. Then create your own custom **PLAN.**

Make use of the four-step format, the example and the resources I provided there, but please don't limit yourself just to them. If necessary, talk to others whom you trust and do additional research to find your own resources that will help you create your own **CUSTOM IDEAL PROFILE** to help you transition from where you are to where you want to be.

All of **Napoleon Hill's** work is excellent, as are books by William Bridges, specifically **Creating You and Co.** and **Managing Transitions**.

## Have at it. Take your time. Create a wonderful Ideal Profile and get ready to meet a new "YOU."

## ~~~IDEAL PROFILE WRITING TIME PASSES~~~

When you're done, please capture your *"Ideal Profile"* thoughts and feelings in your *Learning Journal.*

## ~~ Time passes. ~~

And then it's on to the final section: **In Closing.**

# In Closing

To get to this point, I know you put in a lot of thought, processed a lot of emotions and created your **IDEAL PROFILE** (/ **Ideal / Actual / Obstacles / Plan /**)

And having done that, what you have achieved is AN ACCOMPLISHMENT.

While still fresh in your head and your heart, I encourage you to consider it as **Accomplishment Packet#6** and write it up as you have the others.

If you've done my process as thoroughly as I hope you have, you've faced yourself and thought about and answered a lot of confronting questions. You've **Updated Your Attitude** about yourself and you have **Won Your "Inner Game."**

You've become a *Motivated 10%er.*

You are now ready for *How to Get Interviews! Stop Sending Job Search Junk Mail* where you'll fully develop your **accomplishments, skills** and **Objective statements** so you'll win your **Outer Game and get interviews for meaningful work you want to do.**

You're not quite done.

In order for your *Ideal Profile* to really have a fighting chance to transform your life, there's still some final business around *"YOUR STORY."*

*Learning Journal*

In Chapter 1 and again after you wrote your first Accomplishment Essay in Chapter 5 I asked you to make notes about your *"Story"* and how you would sustain your forward progress. I assume you've been giving that some thought, so these little questions will help you to get your new *"Story"* down on paper.

1.  Write a one-sentence summary of your new *"Story,"* right now. It may help focus your thoughts to think of it as your life's mission statement in one sentence.

2.  Why are you going to the trouble of doing *"all this"* now?

    o   I suggest that the reason you are doing *"all this"* is so you can once-and-for-all **replace your old *"Story"* with a new one that works now and will into the**

**future so you can continue Winning Your _Inner Game_, Your _Outer Game_, interviews, and meaningful work you want to do.**

o   If you have a different reason that is an even stronger _"Why"_ write it all out now

3.   By when will your _"new Story"_ become your _"new reality"_?

4.   What do you have to do to make your _"new reality"_ real?

5.   What do you need to do right now to keep feeling this excited _"New Story"_ feeling next week? Next month?" Forever?

As you answer these questions, please tap into _"POWERFUL EMOTIONS AND POWERFUL MOTIVATIONS."_ Include powerful symbols that are meaningful to you, like my _"Forgiveness Fire"_ stick is to me.

However you choose to answer these final questions, make it safe, meaningful, memorable, and _**cleanse yourself of the toxic sludge of your past that's holding you back.**_

Before you start writing, it will help if you will review your answers to **all the questions in this** _Workbook,_ as well as your completed _**IDEAL PROFILE.**_

**You have now earned the right to write your new _"Story."_**

**Enjoy!**

_Learning Journal._

## ~~~Story Time Passes~~~

And **finally** – here comes your last visit to your _Learning Journal._

You've written your new **"Story."** You've **updated your attitude** and **proven to yourself** _you **can** Win Your "Inner Game."_

## Beyond your Ideal Profile – Your last Learning Journal entry

Andrew Carnegie recognized that for Napoleon Hill to complete his project he was going to need help to keep his focus and stay on track.

You'll recall he gave him this very special affirmation: _**"Andrew Carnegie, I'm not only going to equal your achievements in life, but I'm going to challenge you at the post and pass you at the grandstand."**_

1. In your *Learning Journal,* **write your primary affirmation,** the one that will keep you focused and on-track.

## ~~~Time Passes~~~

You know?

I think you're done with the *Workbook* and with your *Learning Journal* for right now.

You're ready to really learn the **Motivated 10%er** system to make yourself an *"Ideal Candidate"* each time you apply - where it makes sense for you to apply.

**Next step:** your **Motivated 10%er** blueprint - *How to Get Interviews! Stop Sending Job Search Junk Mail* - available on Amazon Kindle and in soft cover on Amazon.com.

## Before you go, may I ask a favor?

Would you please spend a few focused minutes on **www.StopSendingJobSearchJunkMail.com**?

Now that you've become a **Motivated 10%er** I want you to know that on my website you'll find a number of examples of successful targeted résumés and cover letters that people who learned my system have created for themselves. And on my other site, www. YourProfessionalProfile.com, even more targeted Profiles and cover letters that got real results for real people.

You'll also find Amazon links to all of my books.

Finally, while you're there, it would mean a lot to me if you'd sign up for **my blog** (I believe less is more and promise not to fill up your In-Basket with daily or even weekly email).

While on my website, would you also please read about and hopefully join my **10% Army of Converts to help share this process with others who need help to get their work life back on track?**

Other than to wish you the all the best and invite you to **contact me through my website** with questions or to share successes, we're done and you're on your way.

As you look back at how far you've come, know you have my best wishes going forward.

Let me close with a quote from Brendon Burchard's ***The Motivation Manifesto:***

## YOU ARE RESPONSIBLE FOR YOUR REALITY.

## DECIDE WHAT YOU WANT OF THE WORLD AND GO MAKE IT HAPPEN.

## NO CLARITY, NO CHANGE; NO GOALS, NO GROWTH

Don Burrows / The first day of my favorite season - Fall, 2014

# *Free Orientation Coaching Webinar for Purchasers*

*I want to be sure you get off on the right foot.*

*Please click*

*Visit www.StopSendingJobSearchJunkMail.com/Get-Started*

***Your Entry Password is:* Ideal**

# Don't Stop Now

You've learned to **Win Your** *"Inner Game"* and
**"see" yourself** through your
*Relevant Professional Accomplishments*

## NEXT:

*YOU CAN* BE AN
**IDEAL CANDIDATE**
... EACH TIME YOU APPLY

## Here's Your Blueprint

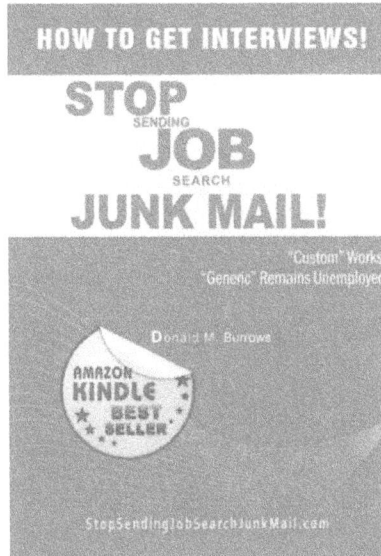
**Available at Amazon.com** – Kindle or Soft-Cover
STAND OUT, LIKE A MEATBALL
Don'tBlendInLikeSpaghetti

# About the Author

**DONALD M. BURROWS**

**Personal Belief:** You CAN be an *"Ideal Candidate"* every time you apply
**Definite Purpose:** Teach people to *"tastefully boast"* and be an *"Ideal Candidate"*
**Personal Code:** Judge by Results. Often harsh. Always fair
**Truth:** *"Through the streets of Bye-and-Bye one arrives at the House of Never"*

Photo by
Sandra Hixon Mathews

My obsession for the last three decades has been helping job seekers, solopreneurs, freelancers and executives-in-transition realize how incredibly competent and powerful they are, and use their accomplishments to stand out like a Meatball on a plate of spaghetti, customize their credentials to each opportunity, present themselves as *"Ideal Candidates"* and win interviews.

My legacy to those who are struggling to get interviews and are being ignored by HR, recruiters and hiring managers is my two-volume set (Amazon Kindle Best Seller ***How to Get Interviews! Stop Sending Job Search Junk Mail*** and its *Companion Workbook*, ***How to Win Your 'Inner Game'. Update Your Attitude Before You 'Update Your Résumé'***).

During 18 years of domestic and international senior Human Resources management, my duties included recruiting and hiring, from entry level to executive, for Marriott Hotels, Chicago Pneumatic Tool Company, Cigna Worldwide, Dole and Chiquita.

One accomplishment of which I'm especially proud:  *When I was Latin American Area HR director for Cigna Worldwide, Corporate decided to centralize their international operations and closed their various Area headquarters. I laid off 90 colleagues and then managed our Corporate in-house outplacement center. I affirm with total certainty that thanks to my interviewing training, résumé-writing and job search strategy skills, all 90 found jobs equal to or better than the ones they lost.*

I hold Bachelor and Master of Arts degrees in Latin American Area Studies and Latin American Literature from the University of Maryland. While you wouldn't know it to look at me, I am native speaker fluent in Spanish. For years I conducted a range of training programs in Spanish and English all over the United States, Europe, Central and South America, the Caribbean and Australia.

Using my system, you'll never again have to mass-post, mass-mail or *"update your résumé"* again because every Professional Profile you submit will be customized to the position's specific requirements – quickly and simply. You'll be an ***"Ideal Candidate"*** each time you apply. And if you are not hired, you'll be able to easily *"repurpose"* your data and be an *"Ideal Candidate"* for new opportunities.

**If you can't get the interview, your education and experience won't matter**

# Also by Donald M. Burrows

Two Serious Topics People Put Off until the Need is On Top of Them

## *1. RÉSUMÉ PREPARATION* / WWW.STOPSENDINGJOBSEARCHJUNKMAIL.COM

### *On Amazon Kindle:*

How to Win Your 'Inner Game'! Update Your Attitude Before You 'Update Your Résumé'(*Companion Workbook* to *How to Get Interviews! Stop Sending Job Search Junk Mail.*). Only 10% of those seeking work have the focus and self-confidence to develop an *"accomplishments mindset,"* and let go of last century's generic reverse-chronological, *"dates-and-duties"* template two-page résumé format (the same format that cherry-picker HR recruiters and hiring managers ignore in favor of those who customize their credentials to each position's specific requirements.) **This *Workbook* is for the remaining 90%** - the ***Generic 90%ers* who present themselves in terms of their dates of employment and job duties and whom recruiters and hiring managers routinely ignore**, even though they are qualified for the opportunities they seek. If you're in this group, this *Companion Workbook* will help you condition your mind to appreciate, know and use your relevant professional accomplishments as the basis to present yourself as an "IDEAL CANDIDATE" each time you apply. You'll revive your self-esteem and give yourself the self-confidence you need so you're ready for *How to Get Interviews! Stop Sending Job Search Junk Mail* Trilogy.

How to Get Interviews! Stop Sending Job Search Junk Mail Trilogy. This is a D-I-Y résumé-writing system; only 10% of job seekers, solopreneurs, freelancers and managers- / executives in transition – the ***Motivated 10%ers*** - are right for this system. Contrary to what you may have been led to believe, you *do* have the ability to write your own résumés and cover letters, and in fact, should. Why? Because employers want to know the *"authentic you,"* not the *"ghost-writer you"* and *you* are the best qualified person to speak on your own behalf. This system is based on your **Representative Professional Accomplishments** and rather than sending out the same generic *"dates-and-duties"* résumé over and over hoping someone will take notice, here you'll learn to create data banks of your most important accomplishments and the skills you used to achieve them. You can customize them to the specific requirements of each opportunity you seek. With your customized résumés, you'll present yourself as an **"Ideal Candidate"** each time you apply, and in the process you'll have prepared yourself to interview effectively.

<u>Overview - How to Get Interviews! Stop Sending Job Search Junk Mail Trilogy</u>. Not sure if you're a good *"fit"* for my system? This **OVERVIEW** will take you no time at all to read and when you're done you'll know two things: you'll understand the three separate elements you must develop to be an IDEAL CANDIDATE and you'll know if you're right for my system.

The Individual Books of the Trilogy. Not everyone needs all three elements of the *Trilogy* but may only need to strengthen one or two of the three legs. Their titles are self-explanatory. Each of the three will lead to greater self-knowledge and the ability to customize that topic so you can *"tastefully boast"* and stand out from your competition, like a meatball stands out on a plate of spaghetti.

<u>"A" is for "Accomplishment"</u>    <u>"S" is for "Skills"</u>    <u>"O" is for "Objective"</u>

### Soft cover on Amazon
<u>How to Get Interviews! Stop Sending Job Search Junk Mail Trilogy</u>.

<u>How to Win Your 'Inner Game' – Update Your Attitude Before You 'Update Your Résumé'</u>(*Companion Workbook* to *How to Get Interviews! Stop Sending Job Search Junk Mail).*

<u>Burn Your Résumé! You Need a Professional Profile: Winning the Inner and Outer Game of Finding Work or New Business</u> (Co-author: Deborah Drake). The precursor to *How to Win Interviews! Stop Sending Job Search Junk Mail,* this book dives deep into detail on both the D-I-Y methodology and how to win your *Inner Game.* And it has an extensive Appendix of real résumés and real cover letters that got real results for real people.

## Available 2Q15 on Amazon and Amazon Kindle

Working title: *Custom Cover Letters! You <u>Can</u> be an* 'Ideal Candidate' *Each Time You Apply!*

## 2. END-OF-LIFE PLANNING / WWW.PLANWHILEYOUSTILLCAN.COM

### On Amazon:

Plan While You Still Can – 16 End-of-Life Checklists You Need Now. **Contains over 400 Yes/No questions to help you know where your current level of End-of-Life Planning is solid and where there are gaps.** ~ To their detriment and that of their families, too many people put off *End-of-Life Planning* until the need is staring them in the face. By then it's too late to do a rational job of what in reality is just another chore that responsible adults take in stride and just do. What I learned about E-L-P I learned first-hand - helping five elders in my family and extended family plan for smooth transitions when the end was in sight. I've learned that legal and financial planning make up only about 20% of a comprehensive *End-of-Life Plan*. People who used this book found it helpful for the obvious 20%, *and invaluable for the other 80%.*

# Connect with Don

Because I welcome the opportunity to connect with you I'm offering a number of avenues for us to do so.

My hope is that together we can sort out the most effective answers to your job search questions and build a community of **Motivated 10%ers** who have successfully used my D-I-Y résumé-writing system and won interviews.

## Facebook Forum

facebook.com/InterviewsGetJobs

This one is brand new. I invite you to be among the first to join. The first 10 enrollees will receive a free 30-minute résumé critique and consultation

## Amazon author's page

www.Amazon.com/Donald-M-Burrows

Amazon graciously provides authors with their own Author Page. This is your link to mine. It is your quick reference to all of my books – current and future

## LinkedIn

https://www.linkedin.com/in/donburrows

A primary source for recruiters and hiring managers, if you're serious about finding meaningful work that is important to you, please take the time to put up an equally serious and complete LinkedIn profile – one that highlights your significant professional accomplishments, and is not just another stagnant and boring rehash chronology of your job dates-and-duties. LinkedIn is a great place to be the meatball, not the spaghetti

## Twitter

twitter.com/DonaldBurrows

Like my Facebook Forum, as you can see, I'm new to Twitter and I'm looking to follow interesting people, do my best to be helpful sharing relevant and interesting Tweets and build a following. Twitter seems like a fine place to do as Garrison Keillor suggests: *"Do good work and keep in touch."*

## StopSendingJobSearchJunkMail.com/Contact

My website contains my <u>contact</u> information, Blog, links to all my books on Amazon. com, thought-provoking examples of D-I-Y résumés and cover letters that real people have created that got them real results, and a link to my <u>10%Army of Converts of *Motivated 10%ers*</u> who have gotten results using my D-I-Y résumé-writing system and want to pay-it-forward by sharing my system with others

# Speaking Engagements and Courses
# (Spanish or English)

1.  90-Minute Introduction to the D-I-Y Professional Profile system

2.  Coaching a four-week two-hours-per-session *Do-It-Yourself résumé-writing course*

***Do-It-Yourself Deliverables:*** D-I-Y Course participants will:

1.  Learn to **Win Their "Inner Game'** by maintaining their self-esteem, focus, self-confidence and composure as they go through the ups and downs of the job search system in today's economy

2.  Stop committing *Generic 90%er Job Search Suicide* - (**"Custom"** Works. **"Generic"** Remains Unemployed.) Stop the insanity of using *"generic résumés"* for *"specific opportunities"*

3.  Develop an *"accomplishments mindset"* to get out of the generic *"applicant pool"* and up onto *"Candidate Slates"* by presenting themselves as *"Ideal Candidates"* for specific positions

4.  Build all the modules of their own custom Professional Profile

5.  Learn to customize (target) their résumés and cover letters to the unique requirements of each position -where it makes sense for them to apply

6.  Use the STAR technique, their custom Professional Profile and the requirements of a real position they are seeking to practice behavioral interviewing

7.  Sidestep much of the competition and stop wasting precious time and energy by no longer engaging in mass-mailings and mass-postings, and by avoiding the *"HR Cattle Chute of No Return"*

8.  Make themselves memorable to recruiters and hiring managers

9.  Learn to think critically about their achievements, and *"tastefully boast"*

10. Identify their *real* special skills and abilities

11. Learn to differentiate between an *"activity"* and an *"accomplishment"*

12. Learn how to confidently and effectively downplay potentially awkward aspects of work history, without resorting to tricks, omissions or deceptions

13. Learn to present themselves authentically so that the person who wrote the cover letter and résumé is the same one on the phone and face-to-face interviews and shows up on Day One for work

**"CUSTOM" Works.**

**"GENERIC" Remains Unemployed.**

# Bonus Tips: 14 Things You Must Do to Be the "Ideal Candidate," win your "Inner Game," and Win Interviews

1. **BE ORIGINAL:** *Avoid fill-in-the-blanks résumé templates.* **WHY? You want your résumé to be an accurate reflection of the authentic "you," not a boring, generic, slapped-together hodge-podge. You want to STAND OUT like a MEATBALL, not blendinlikeforgettablefettuccini**

2. **BE YOURSELF.** *Know that looking for work or new business is like dating.* **WHY? The generic** *"date face"* **is superficial, tiring, unattractive, and gets "old" fast. Show potential employers the authentic "you"**

3. **BE STRATEGIC:** *Stop making it so easy for them to say, "NO!"* **WHY? Help them fall in love with your accomplishments,** *then* **present any negatives, like a problematic job history or lack of a degree**

4. **BE PERSONAL:** *Stop mass-distributing generic résumés, hoping to get lucky.* **WHY? Companies receive thousands of generic** *"spaghetti résumés"* **like yours. Why would they pick yours?**

5. **BE A** *"MEANINGFUL SPECIFIC:"* *Don't be a "wandering generality."* **WHY? Sales trainer legend Zig Ziglar gave the world that wonderful timeless advice. Listen to him and succeed**

6. **BE THE "IDEAL CANDIDATE," NOT JUST ANOTHER VAGUE "GENERIC APPLICANT:"** *Your résumé's job is to get you an interview so you get on the "CANDIDATE SLATE."* **WHY? Because "applicants" can tread water only so long before they drown in the "APPLICANT POOL"**

7. **BE OF CONTRIBUTION:** *The focus of your cover letter and résumé should not be on what* you *want.* **Why? Potential employers and customers want to know what** *you* **can do for** *them* **before they care what you want**

8.   **BE A SOLUTION:** *Use this process to identify your <u>Representative Professional Accomplishments</u> and <u>Special Skills and Abilities.</u>* **WHY? Employers want to know the problems you've fixed for others because they have similar needs**

9.   **BE PROACTIVE:** *To be the Meatball, customize: <u>Objective</u> **then** <u>most relevant Skills</u> **then** <u>Accomplishments</u>.* **WHY? You have only 5–7 seconds to win reader interest, or you're toast**

10.  **BE DISRUPTIVE:** *Put yourself in the hiring manager's shoes.* **WHY? Which would catch your eye first and make you want to read: a generic dates-and-duties** *"spaghetti"* **résumé OR the accomplishments and skills MEATBALL, customized to the requirements of your position?**

11.  **BE IN INTEGRITY:** *Don't mislead by trying to appear younger.* **Why? Effectively presented, your accomplishments speak for you. Deceit is unnecessary, unworthy, and embarrassing**

12.  **BE CONGRUENT:** *"Imagine having a résumé that gets you an interview, but giving an interview that makes them wonder why they invited you in."* **WHY?** *"The same "person" who sends in their credentials should be the same one who shows up for the interviews and starts work on Day One."* **- Deborah Drake, co-author of** *Burn Your Résumé! You Need a Professional Profile.*

13.  **BE UNIQUE:** *"CUSTOM" works. "GENERIC" remains unemployed.* **WHY? This is an Employer's Market and they have thousands of "Custom" résumés to choose from. To put it very bluntly, they won't give the GENERIC JOB SEARCH JUNK MAIL you mass-distribute a second glance. They'll ignore you, like you ignore junk mail at home**

14.  **BE "RESPONSE-ABLE:"** *Lose the "Victim" story.* **WHY? No one wants to hire a "victim," and in this labor market, they don't need to and they won't. YOU are keeping yourself unemployed.**

# One last thing

Interviews lead to jobs.

I hope this *Workbook* will help you win the interviews that will lead to meaningful work you want to do.

If you've become a ***Motivated 10%er*** and you believe what you've learned here will help you **win your** *"Inner Game,"* please review it on Amazon.com.

I hope you loved it, but loved it or hated it, your comments will help me make future editions even better.

Thank you. Very much.

To your success!